THE PROBATE HANDBOOK

Tim Bracken

Margaret Campbell

Published by
Clarus Press Ltd,
Griffith Campus,
South Circular Road,
Dublin 8.

Typeset by
Marsha Swan

Printed by
CPI Group (UK) Ltd,
Croydon,
CR0 4YY

ISBN
978-1-905536-38-2
Reprinted 2012

Disclaimer
Whilst every effort has been made to ensure that the contents of this book are accurate, neither the publisher nor author can accept responsibility for any errors or omissions or loss occasioned to any person acting or refraining from acting as result of any material in this publication.

Dedicated to the memory of Alfie Campbell who,
during his years in the Probate Registry in Cork,
was of great assistance to numerous practitioners

Foreword

I am pleased to write the foreword to this book.

Probate practice can be intricate, detailed, challenging and anything but straightforward. It requires a comprehensive knowledge and understanding of the law and of the relevant procedures involved in obtaining Grants of Representation.

This book is written in a very clear style with the obvious intention of assisting practitioners in resolving the problems that may arise. As well as dealing with the many relevant statutes, it also gives worthwhile information on the varied procedures to be used and contains both forms and precedents which will assist in the extraction of various Grants.

The authors are to be congratulated for their diligence and work in producing this publication. I recommend it to both practitioners and students and I wish it the success it deserves.

Patrick Moran
The Circuit Court
Cork
April 2011

Preface

Probate practice is not confined to the administration of estates of deceased persons. It also encompasses the drafting of Wills, advising on Capital Acquisitions Tax and dealing with court applications and proceedings against estates under the Succession Act or matters of a testamentary nature.

This book is written with the practitioner in mind. It is designed to be a reference book providing quick solutions and guidelines to various procedures which arise in relation to probate matters.

Practitioners must be very careful when drafting Wills and should certainly advise the testator as to what may or may not happen if certain provisions are inserted in a Will. There is also a duty of care to beneficiaries named in the Will to ensure that the Will is valid.

The book also deals with various Court applications, both contentious and non-contentious which may be necessary and it is designed as a handbook for the practitioner rather than an exhaustive treatise.

It gives an overview in relation to Capital Acquisitions Tax and the main points which may arise in the administration of the estate and also in relation to discretionary trusts.

The text incorporates the changes brought about by the Finance Act 2010 in relation to the payment of Capital Acquisitions Tax and the filing of the Inland Revenue Affidavit in the Probate Office.

We would like to thank David McCartney, our publisher, for his patience and advice and also Tim's daughter, Lydia Bracken for help in research.

We have endeavoured to state the law as of November 2010.

We hope the work fulfils the need of the busy Probate practitioner. We have set it out in a simple user friendly style which will enable the practitioner to access and source the law, cases and materials pertinent to Probate practice in an easy and efficient manner.

April 2011
Tim Bracken
Margaret Campbell

Table of Contents

Chapter 1

Introduction

The greatest inevitability of life is that we all die at some stage and therefore every person dies either having made a Will ("testate"), or without a Will ("intestate").

Testate

A person is said to die "testate" if they leave behind them a valid document (known as a Will) giving directions as to the distribution of their estate which comprises their assets and properties, both real and personal.

Their estate is then distributed in accordance with their wishes as outlined in their Will, subject to any claims by a spouse or civil partner for a legal right share, or children under s 117 of the Succession Act 1965.

Intestate

A person is said to die "intestate" when they die without leaving a Will. The estate of an intestate is distributed in accordance with the provisions of the laws in force at the time and the estate may be distributed in a manner which the deceased person did not envisage, but due to the fact that they did not execute a Will prior to death, the law takes over and the distribution is in accordance with the provisions of whatever Act is in force at the date of their death.

Relevant Succession Acts

1. The Succession Act 1965 (27 of 1965) which came into operation on the 1st January 1967.

2. The Administration of Estates Act 1959 (8 of 1959), which was repealed in whole by the Succession Act 1965, is still relevant for deaths between the 1st June 1959 and the 31st December 1966 inclusive.

3. The Intestates Estate Act 1954 (12 of 1954), which in whole was repealed by the Succession Act 1965, still applies to deaths between the 1st June 1954 and the 31st December 1966.

4. The Rules of the Superior Courts (RSC) 1986, SI No. 15 of 1986, Order 79.

5. The Rules of the Circuit Court (RCC) 2001, SI No. 510 Order 50.

It should be borne in mind that notwithstanding the fact that the Intestates Estate Act 1954 and the Administration of Estates Act 1959 are both repealed in full, both Acts are still relevant if the practitioner is dealing with a death which occurred in the periods as outlined above. This will generally happen when the practitioner is seeking to extract a second grant known as a "*de bonis non* grant" in an older estate in order to rectify something in a title and the provisions of these Acts should be noted. However, it regularly happens that one is instructed to administer an estate where the death was "pre Succession Act", that is prior to the 1st January 1967.

The date of death is the defining date as to which enactment applies to the estate and this is also very important from a capital acquisitions tax ("CAT") aspect. The date of death will define the periods of aggregation of prior gifts and the amount of the group threshold applicable. See chapter 10 below.

Duties of executors and administrators: It is the duty of every executor and administrator to administer the estate of the deceased in accordance with the terms of the will or the provisions of the Succession Act 1965. These duties include extracting the grant, marshalling the assets, discharging the debts and distributing the assets.

National Private Property Registration NPPR

Since the commencement of the Local Government (Charges) Act 2009 all residential property which is not occupied by the owner as his or her sole or main residence is subject to a charge on that property. This charge is commonly known as the second property charge. If the charge is not paid on the due date penalties are applied and are a charge on the property.

In relation to property of a deceased which has not yet been vested in a beneficiary the local authority are charging the property with the charge from the date of the grant and regard the personal representatives as the persons with liability for the charge until the property is vested in the beneficiary. Practitioners should be aware of this and advise accordingly.

Chapter 2

Grants of Representation and Administration of Estates

Introduction

This chapter will explain the procedures for making an application to the Probate Office or District Probate Registry for a Grant of Representation in the estate of a deceased person.

In the normal day to day running of a practice, the practitioner will come across six types of application and each type will be dealt with separately. The term "legal personal representative" is used to describe anyone to whom a Grant of Representation in the estate of a deceased person issues.

The Six Types of Grants of Representation

1. **Grant of Probate:** This grant issues to an executor named in a Will who is alive and willing to act.

2. **Grant of Administration with the Will Annexed:** This grant issues when a Will has been made and someone other than an executor acts as legal personal representative.

3. **Grant of Administration Intestate:** This grant issues when a deceased dies without having made a Will.

4. **Second or Subsequent Grants:** This grant issues when the original grant that issued is no longer valid – for example on the death of the original legal personal representative.

5. **Limited Grant:** This grant issues when a grant is to be limited in duration (when the person entitled to the grant is a minor), or where needed to institute proceedings or to cover a trust property.

6. **Special Grant:** Sometimes a grant is issued pursuant to an Order under s 27(4) of the Succession Act. This section allows the court to issue a grant in certain circumstances to a person who would not, under the normal rules of succession, be otherwise entitled to act as administrator of an estate.

Inland Revenue Affidavit

For all Grants of Representation the preparation and swearing of an Inland Revenue Affidavit is mandatory. The filing of an Inland Revenue Affidavit with the Revenue Commissioners for certification, in advance of applying to the High Court Probate Office for a Grant of Representation in a deceased person's estate was a long established practice. However, from June 2010, where a deceased person died on or after the 5th of December 2001, this practice was replaced by a new procedure.

Inland Revenue Affidavit: For deaths which have occurred since 2001 the Inland Revenue affidavit is no longer certified by the Revenue prior to the application for the Grant of Representation.

The affidavit for deaths post 2001 can be downloaded from the Revenue site http://www.revenue.ie/en/tax/cat/forms/index.html and completed as directed, or it can be filled out on a pre printed form that is available directly from the CAT Office. If the pre printed form is used, then a blue biro must be used. The affidavit is to be completed in duplicate (not photocopied) and the two copies form part of the application for the Grant of Representation to the Probate Office/Probate Registry. The Probate Office/Probate Registry deals directly with the Revenue Commissioners following the lodging of the application for the grant.

All fields in the affidavit are mandatory and failure to complete them will result in the affidavit being rejected by the Probate Office/District Probate Registry.

Both affidavits must be signed by the applicant/applicants and sworn by the commissioner/practising solicitor in the usual way.

The affidavit is submitted directly to the Probate Office/Registry with all the other necessary documentation for the Grant of Representation in the deceased's estate.

The Probate Office/District Probate Registry will check the Inland Revenue affidavit insofar as the probate element of the process is concerned. All tax details will become a matter in due course for the Revenue Commissioners.

When the grant issues in the estate in question, the Grant of Representation no longer has a certificate thereon indicating the position regarding the payment or otherwise of the Capital Acquisitions Tax.

A certificate indicating the delivery of an Inland Revenue affidavit in the estate, together with the gross and net value of the estate, appears on the face of the grant when it issues from the Probate Office/Registry.

Once the Grant of Representation issues in the deceased person's estate:

(a) one of the duplicate Inland Revenue affidavits already furnished to the Probate Office/Registry will be forwarded to the Revenue Commissioners by the Probate Office/Registry.

(b) Details regarding the issue of the Grant of Representation and other relevant information as is held in electronic form by the Probate Office/Registry will be transmitted electronically to the Revenue Commissioners.

For second or subsequent grants for deaths post 2001 the Revenue forms must be filed in duplicate with the application to the Probate Office/Registry.

Inland Revenue pre 2001: the old procedures apply and the affidavit has to be certified by the CAT Office before application is made to the Probate Office/Registry. For applications for second or subsequent grants for deaths prior to 2001 the Revenue forms are filed with the Revenue before making the application for the grant.

Grant of Probate

When the deceased has died testate and has named an executor then this person has priority to deal with the administration of the estate. An executor appointed under a Will does not have to act: he or she can reserve or renounce the right to act and, should this occur, the grant raised will be a Grant of Administration with the Will annexed. Should one of a number of executors reserve or renounce his rights and another executor remains on as executor, then the grant to be applied for is a Grant of Probate with the matter of the reservation or renouncing of rights dealt with in the body of the oath. However, it should be pointed out that, once a Grant of Probate issues the legal personal representative cannot renounce his office without leave of the High Court.

Where more than one executor is appointed, one or more can apply for the Grant of Probate reserving the rights of the others to act. Where a sole executor is appointed, reservation of the rights is not possible. While the proving executor does not have a legal duty to notify the other executor that he intends to "reserve" the rights of the other executor/executors, it is prudent and preferable to obtain a letter confirming the position.

For practical purposes, it is better for a non acting executor to reserve his rights rather than to renounce, in that the reservation is merely referred to in the oath while a renunciation is an actual form that has to be signed by the renouncing executor and marked as an exhibit in the oath by the applicant for the Grant and the commissioner who is marking the Oath, Bond and Will. It is important to remember that the same commissioner must mark all the papers for the application. It need not be the same commissioner who marks the Inland Revenue affidavit for the application.

While on the face of it a Grant of Probate is probably the easiest to apply for, nonetheless a significant number of applications are rejected by the Probate Office due to errors in forms making up the application.

Under the Rules of the Superior Court 1986, applications to the Probate Office must be made personally or through town agents. The Probate Office does not accept applications by post. However, postal applications are accepted by District Probate Registries.

The documents necessary for the application to either the District Probate Registry (that is the district where the deceased resided) or the Probate Office are as follows:

1. *The Inland Revenue Affidavit* completed by the solicitor acting in the administration of the estate, signed by the applicant and sworn in the usual way but note the changes in procedure as detailed above. Where land forms part of the estate, a form CA6 is also required.

2. *Original Will* with the signature of the Executor and witnessing Commissioner for Oaths/Practising Solicitor on the back and a copy thereof (three copies in the case of applications to the District Registries)

3. *Oath for Executor and a copy thereof (two when lodging application in local Registries).* Make sure the oath for Executor is correctly completed and that the gross value of the assets as per the *Inland Revenue Affidavit* is detailed. The names and addresses of the deceased and the executors as contained in the oath must be as set out in the Will. All variations must be referred to and where the address of either the deceased or executor has

changed, then the oath must cover both addresses. The oath is to be dated no earlier than six months prior to the application and the same Commissioner for Oath/Practising Solicitor is to witness the signature of the executor on the oath and back of the Will.

4. *Probate Office Fees* based on net estate as certified in Inland Revenue Affidavit located on the Courts Service site.

5. *Death Certificate of the deceased.*

6. *Renunciation of Executor (See appendix A Precedents) (if applicable).*

7. *Resolution of Trust Corporation (if applicable).*

Possible Extra Documents

In addition to the above it may be necessary to file one or more affidavits to complete the application. The most common are: Affidavits of Attesting Witness; Affidavits of Plight and Condition; and Affidavits of Mental Capacity.

Affidavit of Attesting Witness

An Affidavit of Attesting Witness will be necessary if the "attestation clause" is in any way defective. The attestation clause is the clause at the end of the Will where it is confirmed that the testator has signed the Will and that it has been witnessed by two witnesses.

It is a prerequisite of s 78 of the Succession Act 1965 that, in order for a Will to be valid, it must be validly executed. For this reason it is very important to remember the provisions of s 78 at the Will drafting state. If these formalities are properly complied with then such affidavits may not in fact be required. Section 78 deals with the form and execution of a Will and is a section well worth being familiar with.

An Affidavit of Attesting Witness will also be required where the testator signs with a mark, being unable to write due to illiteracy or physical infirmity, or where the signature is feeble, indecipherable or poorly formed, or is blind. In these situations the affidavit should state the reason for the poor signature or mark and should confirm that the Will was read to or by the testator prior to execution and that the testator was of sound disposing mind (see forms no 5, 7 and 9 in chapter 12 below).

Affidavit of Plight and Condition
An Affidavit of Plight and Condition will be necessary if the Will/Codicil is damaged in any way (for example torn or has staple marks and so on) or has been executed on separate sheets that have not been bound prior to execution. A solicitor familiar to dealing with probate files will generally realise when an Affidavit of Plight and Condition will be required by looking at the physical condition of the Will. The affidavit must show how the marks or tears, etc. occurred and must state that nothing of a testamentary nature was at any time attached to the said Will/Codicil (see form no 9 in chapter 12 below).

Affidavit of Mental Capacity
An Affidavit of Mental Capacity will be required if a cause of death on the Death Certificate refers in any way to mental disease (for example Alzheimers Disease). This affidavit is to be completed by the medical practitioner attending the deceased at the time of execution of the Will (see forms no 5 and 6 in chapter 12 below).

Charitable Bequest Form
A Charitable Bequest Form is required when the Will contains any gift of a charitable nature.

No Affidavit of Market Value is required for an application for a Grant of Probate.

In cases where you are doubtful as to whether an affidavit is required, and to avoid the application being rejected by the Probate Office, it may be prudent to check before lodging whether a particular affidavit will be required.

Grant of Administration with the Will Annexed

When a person dies testate, but someone other than an executor is to administer the estate, then the grant applied for is a Grant of Administration with the Will Annexed.

These Grants arise where:

No executor has been named in the Will or where appointment of executor is void due to uncertainty;

Where named executor/executors have died without proving the Will;

Where the executor/executors have either renounced or have been deemed to renounce on foot of an application by an interested party;

Where the executor is under a disability – due to age, mental capacity or is a body not considered to be a trust corporation;

The person most often entitled to take out a Grant of Administration with the Will Annexed is the universal residuary legatee and devisee. The order of entitlement is quite easy to work out and it is a question of getting used to reading the residuary clauses and working from there.

The order of entitlement is as follows:

The Universal or Residuary legatee or devisees in trust – but never their personal representatives;

The Universal or Residuary legatee or devisee who is entitled to the share absolutely;

The Universal or Residuary legatee or devisees for life – again their legal personal representatives can never take out the grant;

The Residuary legatee or devisee in remainder; this is where the remainder of the estate will devolve on the death of someone who has been given a life interest under the residue;

Person entitled on intestacy where no residue clause is contained in the Will or if the residue has lapsed;

The legal personal representative of the beneficial universal or residuary legatee or devisee who has survived the deceased and who has since died without proving the Will or the legal personal representative of the person entitled on intestacy;

The legatee or devisee – only on the renunciation of the universal/residuary legatee and devisee;

A Creditor of the estate – allowed to apply on foot of court Order or Order of the Probate Officer;

The State – where the person dies partially or wholly intestate without any known relative and nobody having any interest in the estate.

The oath must clear off any person with prior entitlement to the taking out of the grant and precedents are contained in the appendix to this handbook.

For deaths prior to the 1st of June 1959, the devisee (whether universal, residuary, beneficial or in trust) need not be cleared off.

The residue of an estate is what is left over after specific gifts of property have been made. A specific gift will not constitute a gift of the residue even though it comprises all the estate of the estate. The estate is deemed to have something left to be disposed of and, in the absence of a residuary clause, the "residue" will go on intestacy.

Residuary Devisee is the person to whom the residue of any real estate is left.

Residuary Legatee is the person to whom the residue of the personal estate is left.

Joint Residuary Legatees or Devisees must apply together or if one applies, the others must consent to the application. Where they take as tenants in common then any one of them can apply – without reference to the others being made. On the death of them all, the legal personal representative of any may apply.

Documents necessary to lodge an application for Grant of Administration with the Will Annexed:

1. Death Certificate.

2. Original Will (and Codicil if executed) to be marked by applicant and Commissioner/Solicitor. Where the Will has been proved in another jurisdiction, a copy of the Will sealed and certified by the court where it was proved is to be marked by the applicant and the commissioner – a sealed and certified copy of the Grant which issued in that jurisdiction must also be lodged.

3. Engrossment of Will and Codicil (three copies if application is to local registry) and certified by solicitor acting.

4. Oath for Administrator with the Will Annexed and copy thereof (two copies required if application is to local registry). Heading to include the name, address and former addresses and occupation (note particularly the address in the deceased's Will). As already stated, the oath must clear off prior interests and show clearly how the applicant has come to be entitled to apply for the grant. The estate is to be split into real and personal estate – which includes leasehold property – and the current value of immovable property is to be used rather than the value as at the date of death which is the value used for movable property.

5. Inland Revenue Affidavit and CA6 (for lands and buildings) giving date of death values of the assets – note the changes cited above regarding the filing of the Inland Revenue Affidavit.

6. Bond – penal sum to cover double the gross assets (including *current* value of any land); applicant to execute bond before same Commissioner/Solicitor before whom oath was sworn – if not, an Order must be obtained from the Probate Officer allowing different Commissioners/Solicitors on oath and bond. The clause dealing with the filing of the Will if found, is to be deleted. For deaths prior to 1 June 1959 a different form of bond is to be used and another form again for deaths between 1 June 1959 and 31 December 1966.

The title must be shown – not the blood relationship (e.g. the residuary legatee and devisee/lawful spouse).

Letter or Affidavit of Current Market Value – letter from solicitor certifying current market value will suffice unless property is of a commercial or agricultural nature and where property comprises of more than one acre.

7. Affidavit of Attesting Witness – always required where there is no or a defective attestation clause; blind or illiterate testator – to confirm that the Will was read over to the testator prior to execution; the Will was written on front side only of paper and attestation clause does not confirm number of pages. All affidavits should confirm due execution.

8. Affidavit of Plight and Condition – required where tear marks, pinholes, paperclips, etc. appear on Will.

9. Affidavit of Mental Capacity – required where testator was a Ward of Court, suffered from a mental illness or died resident in a mental institution. This affidavit is to be sworn by the medical doctor attending the deceased at the time the Will was executed.

10. Charitable Bequest Form – required where there are charitable bequests in the Will

11. Probate Office Fees will depend on the net estate as shown in the Inland Revenue affidavit and can be obtained from the Courts Service site.

Grant of Administration Intestate

Where a person dies without having made a valid Will, he is said to have died intestate and his estate will be distributed in accordance with Part VI of the Succession Act 1965. Before distribution of the estate can take place, however, a Grant of Letters of Administration Intestate may need to be extracted in the estate. While the Succession Act sets out who is entitled to share in the intestate's estate, the Rules of the Superior Court 1986 determine who is entitled to apply for the grant. It follows that an entitlement to apply for a Grant of Letters of Administration Intestate invariably follows a right to take a share in the estate on an intestacy.

Two main points to remember are:

1. The interest is established at date of death
2. The grant follows the interest.

Interest is Established at Date of Death

It is important to remember when taking instructions in relation to an intestacy that the entitlement to extract the Grant of Administration Intestate is determined conclusively at the date of death of the deceased – this is provided for by s 71 of the Succession Act which states that "the person or persons who, at the date of death of the intestate stand nearest in blood relationship to him, shall be taken to be his next of kin".

Relatives of the half blood have the same entitlement as relatives of the whole blood. However, step relatives have no entitlement to succeed to an intestate estate or to apply for the grant.

Non marital relations are entitled to apply following the enactment of the Status of Children Act 1987 where the deceased died after 14 June 1988 and adopted children can apply under the terms of the Adoption Act 1952.

Grant Follows the Interest

This is a very important concept and once grasped makes life much easier for practitioners. It means that the nearest next of kin alive at the date of death of the intestate deceased are entitled to inherit the estate (and therefore apply for the grant).

The rules governing the entitlement to apply for a grant in these circumstances are contained in Order 79, Rule 5(1) of the Rules of the Superior Court (as amended) and apply to deaths that occur after 1 January 1967:

> "The persons having a beneficial interest in the estate of the deceased shall be entitled to a Grant of Administration in the following order of priority, namely:
>
> (a) the surviving spouse;
>
> (b) the surviving spouse jointly with a child of the deceased nominated by the said spouse;

(c) the child or children of the deceased (including any person entitled by virtue of the Status of Children Act 1987 to succeed to the estate of the deceased);

(d) the issue of any child who has died during the lifetime of the deceased;

(e) the father or mother of the deceased;

(f) brothers and sisters of the deceased (whether of the whole or half blood);

(g) where any brother or sister survived the deceased and who has since died the children of a predeceased brother or sister;

(h) nephews or nieces of the deceased (whether of the whole or half blood);

(i) grand parents;

(j) uncles or aunts (whether of the whole or half blood);

(k) great grand parents;

(l) other next of kin of nearest degree (whether of the whole or half blood), preferring collaterals to direct lineal ancestors – first cousins, great uncles or aunts, grand nephews and grand nieces, great great grand parents;

(m) nominee of the State – in such a case the AG usually nominates the Chief State Solicitor to take out the grant although he does have power to make any nomination he wishes."

Where more than one person falls into a class of those entitled to apply for a grant, any member of that class can apply without reference to any others equally entitled. If there are conflicting claims for a grant among the members of a class equally entitled, the grant shall be made to such of the applicants as the Probate Office shall select, having first given not less than twenty one days' notice to the rival claimant or, on an objection made in writing within the twenty one day period, to such person as the court shall select.

No Grant of Administration Intestate shall be issued jointly to more than three persons unless the Probate Office otherwise directs. Thus if a large class of persons are equally entitled to take out the grant, for example four nephews and five nieces, then it is better practice to have them nominate one of the group who will extract the grant and have them confirm this in writing.

Documents Required When Applying for a Grant of Letters of Administration Intestate

The following documents must be lodged in the Probate Office or in the District Probate Registry as appropriate:

1. Death Certificate (or copy thereof);

2. Oath for Administrator Intestate (with copy thereof for Probate Office and two copies when lodged in District Registry);

3. Bond;

4. Inland Revenue Affidavit (see notes above re new procedures);

5. Affidavit of Current Market Value (or letter of Current Market Value as appropriate).

Oath of Administrator Intestate

The Oath of Administrator Intestate sets out the entitlement of the applicant to extract the grant. It contains the name, address and occupation of the deceased and all variations (as per the Death Certificate) should be set out in this document. As the oath proves the right of the applicant to take out the grant, the title is worded so as to "clear off" all persons with prior entitlement to the grant.

The oath must refer separately to the value of the real (freehold land) and the personal property (all other assets of the deceased). Furthermore it is the gross current value of the real property that must be stated.

The title of the applicant in the oath is of paramount importance and a number of precedent titles for death intestate after the 1st of January 1967 are listed below:

Husband or Widow: "Died intestate a married man/woman. I am the lawful widow/widower";

Child of a Married Man: "Died intestate a married man whose widow "A" has died (or who has renounced her rights (exhibit renunciation)) and I am the lawful son/daughter";

Child of Married Woman: "Died intestate a married woman whose husband "B" has died (or who has renounced his rights (exhibit renunciation) and I am the lawful son/daughter";

Child of Widow or Widower: "Died intestate a widow/widower and I am the lawful son/daughter";

Grandchild: "Died intestate a widow/widower without children and I am the lawful grandchild";

Father or Mother: "Died intestate a bachelor/spinster (or widow/widower) without child, grandchild or other descendant, and I am the lawful mother/father";

Brother or Sister: "Died intestate a bachelor/spinster (or widow/widower) without issue or parent and I am the lawful brother or sister";

Nephew or Niece: "Died intestate a bachelor (or spinster etc.) without issue, or parent, brother or sister and I am the lawful niece/nephew";

Grandparent: "Died intestate a bachelor (or spinster etc) with issue, parent, brother or sister or nephew or niece and that I am the lawful grandmother/grandfather";

Uncle or Aunt: "Died intestate a bachelor (or spinster etc.) without issue, parent, brother or sister, nephew or niece or grandparent and that I am the lawful aunt/uncle";

First Cousin: "Died intestate a bachelor (or spinster etc.) without issue, parent, brother or sister, nephew or niece, grandparent, uncle or aunt, or great grandparent and that I am the lawful first cousin";

First Cousin Once Removed "Died a bachelor (or spinster etc) with issue or parent or other lineal ancestor, brother or sister, nephew or niece, or descendant of such, uncle or aunt in any degree or first cousin and that I am the first cousin once removed";

Representative of a Child: "Died a widow/widower with grandchild or other descendant who would have been the issue of a predeceased child and leave her/him surviving two lawful and only children "A" who has since died and "B" who has renounced her rights (exhibit renunciation) and that I am the legal personal representative of the said "A" under Grant of Probate (other Grant) which issued forth to me from the Probate Office/District Probate Registry at Cork (etc) on the day of;

Representative of Brother or Sister: "Died a bachelor/spinster without issue or parent or nephew or niece who would have been the issue of a predeceased brother or sister and leaving him/her surviving one lawful and only brother "A" who lawful and only sisters "B" and "C", all of whom have since died and that I am the legal personal representative of the said A under Grant of Probate (etc.) that issued forth to me, etc;

Issue of a Predeceased Child – Surviving Child Renouncing: "Died intestate a married man/woman leaving him/her surviving his lawful widow/widower A who has since died and one lawful and only child "B" who has renounced his rights (exhibit renunciation) and that I am the lawful son/daughter of "C" who was a lawful child of and who predeceased the deceased";

Issue of Predeceased Brother or Sister: "Died a bachelor (or widower etc.) without issue or parent, leaving one lawful and only brother "A" and one lawful and only sister "B" both of whom have since died and that I am the lawful son/daughter of "C" who was a lawful brother/sister of and who predeceased the deceased.

Second or Subsequent Grants
(commonly known as *De Bonis Non Grants*)

De bonis non Grants are necessary if the estate has not been fully administered on the death of the legal personal representative of the original Grant. There are two types of *de bonis non Grants* – Grant of Administration *de bonis non* and Grant of Administration with the Will Annexed *de bonis non*.

Where the original Grant is one of Administration the person entitled to extract the Grant of Adminisration *de bonis non* is someone of equal standing to the original administrator. If, however, there is no person of equal standing, then the correct applicant is the next entitled in the line of succession.

Straightforward examples of titles in the Oath for a Grant of Administration *de bonis non* are:

> X died intestate a married man/married woman whose widow/widower Y extracted a Grant of Administration from the Probate on the ____ day of ____ and who has since on the ____ day of ____ without completing the administration of the estate; and I am the lawful son/daughter, etc;

> X died a bachelor/spinster without parent whose brother/sister Y extracted a Grant of Administration from the Probate Office on the ____ day of ____ and has since died on the ____ day of ____ without complet-

ing the administration of the estate and I am the lawful brother/sister, etc. …

The per stirpes rule regarding issue of predeceased children and issue of predeceased brothers and sisters may have to be taken into account when calculating the entitlement to take out de bonis non Grants.

A Grant of Administration with the Will annexed *de bonis non* is taken out when a Will has been proved either by way of Grant of Probate and the personal representative has died leaving no other executor to act. The Grant is given the next entitled – the residuary legatee and devisee and if none the rules attaching to entitlement generally under a Will apply. Where the original Grant extracted was a Grant of Administration with the Will annexed and again the original personal representative has died without completing the administration of the estate, then the *de bonis* Grant is taken out by the next entitled.

Straightforward examples of the title in the Oath are:

and did therein name as his sole executor Y who extracted a Grant of Probate from the Probate Office in Dublin on the _____ day of _____ and who has since died on the _____ day of _____ without completing the administration of the estate and I am the residuary legatee and devisee named in the said Will etc. …

and did not therein name any executor and did therein name as his residuary legatee and devisee Y who extracted a Grant of Administration with the Will Annexed from the Probate Office on the _____ day of _____ and who has since died on the _____ day of _____ without completing the administration of the estate and I am the legal personal representative of the said Y under Grant of Probate/Administration/ W.A. that issued forth to me from the Probate Office on the ____ day of ____ etc. …

It is important to remember that the *de bonis non* Grant has to be applied for to the same Probate Registry/Office as the original grant – unless the original grant issued prior to 1 January 1967 when all subsequent grants must be applied for in the Probate Office.

The forms used are similar are for the original grants but the title in the oath will be amended as necessary.

The Revenue form is the A3 which can be downloaded and again does not have to be certified by the Revenue if death is prior to 2001. Only the unadministered estate is accounted for in the schedule. The value in the oath is the current value of freehold property and leasehold property. The value is again doubled in the bond. The word "unadministered" is inserted every place the word "estate" is used.

The original grant (or sealed and certified copy if not available) must be lodged with the application.

Where a Will is involved the original grant (or sealed and certified copy) is to be exhibited in the oath (marked by applicant and commissioner).

Chapter 3

Wills

A Will is a solemn document in writing executed by a person giving directions as to the distribution of his/her estate after their death.

Requirements for a Valid Will

The requirements for a valid Will are set out in ss 77 and 78 of the Succession Act 1965 and are as follows:

1. The Will must be in writing and executed in accordance with the rules set out in s 78.

2. The testator must be over 18 or is, or has been, married.

3. The testator must be of sound disposing mind.

Taking Instructions for a Will

A solicitor, when taking instructions from a client in respect of a proposed Will, should ensure that s/he has the following information as this will be required for the Will and should advise as outlined:

a. Name and address of testator.

b. Details of any previous Wills. It should be explained to the client that the execution of a new Will will revoke any previous Will and therefore the new Will is effectively starting from scratch.

c. Whether the client has been or is married or in a civil partnership and if s/he is single or plans to marry or enter into a civil partnership in the future it should be pointed out to him/her that a Will is revoked on the subsequent marriage or entry into a civil partnership of the Testator unless a contrary intentions appears in the Will.

d. Appointment of executors and if a trust is to be created in the will, trustees. If the clients are a couple whether married or not and have young children they should be advised to appoint trustees and guardians of the children, in the event of them both dying contemporaneously. The appointment of trustees and guardians of infant children should be strongly advised. It is very important that it is stressed to them that they should discuss this with the proposed trustees and guardians. Quite often they will appoint one from his family and one from her family and that may not be of much use to the children if these are two separate families. It is a matter to which the couple should give a lot of consideration and they should be clear as to whom they wish to appoint. Furthermore, they should not appoint somebody without having fully discussed the matter with the proposed guardian/trustee. If the trust is one which might be caught by the definition of a discretionary trust then the testator should be advised of the implication of that type of trust. See chapter 9 "Discretionary Trust".

e. The solicitor who has drafted the Will may be appointed executor of the Will. However, for that solicitor who is appointed executor to be entitled to charge for his legal services in the administration of the estate at a later stage, there must be a charging clause in the Will. An appropriate charging clause such as the following should be inserted in the Will.

> "I hereby direct that my solicitor _____(name) may charge the appropriate fees for the administration of my estate notwithstanding the fact that he is named as executor of this my will"

In such cases the Solicitor should not then witness the Will.

f. Provisions as to the disposal of property. The testator should be clear as to the division of his or her property. After the testator has given a list of his instructions to the solicitor as to the disposal of the property, the testator should be advised if the proposed disposal may give rise to potential litigation at a later stage. If the testator is proposing to leave a spouse or a civil partner less than a legal right share he should be advised that during the administration of the estate the executor has a duty to inform the spouse or a civil partner of their right to be put on an election between accepting the legal right share or the bequest under the Will pursuant to s 115 of the Succession Act 1965. Furthermore if the testator is either disinheriting or favouring one child over another then he should be advised of the provisions of s 117 of the Succession Act 1965. The testator should also be advised that in the event of litigation occurring in relation to the estate generally, the costs of such litigation are borne by the residue of the estate and consequently it is the residuary legatees who will ultimately bear the costs.

g. A testator who is not leaving a spouse or a civil partner the equivalent of the legal right share or indeed the
dwellinghouse, should be informed of the provisions of
s 56 of the Succession Act 1965 which confers a right
on the surviving spouse or a civil partner to require the
dwellinghouse and the household chattels to be appropriated in satisfaction of the legal right share as this may
conflict with the testator's wishes.

The testator should be informed of these matters and it
should be pointed out that if the provisions of the sections
are ignored, this may result in the estate being tied up in litigation subsequent to the death of the testator (see page 79 for
full text of s 115).

h. Advancements: In relation to bequests to children, full
instructions should be taken from the testator in relation to any prior gifts or advancements made to a child
during the lifetime of the testator. It should be pointed
out to the testator that the expression "advancement" is
defined in s 63(6) of the Succession Act 1965 as follows:

63.—(6) For the purposes of this section, "advancement"
means a gift intended to make permanent provision for a
child and includes advancement by way of portion or settlement, including any life or lesser interest and including
property covenanted to be paid or settled. It also includes
an advance or portion for the purpose of establishing a child
in a profession, vocation, trade or business, a marriage portion and payments made for the education of a child to a
standard higher than that provided by the deceased for any
other or others of his children.

If any of the prior gifts or dispositions to the children come within the ambit of that definition, the testator should then be informed that such advancements can be ignored by inserting an appropriate clause into the Will and the child who received the advancement will then be on an equal footing with the other siblings subsequent to the death of the testator. An appropriate clause could be as follows:

> "I hereby declare that any prior gifts or dispositions which come within the definition of advancement as contained in Section 63 of the Succession Act 1965 shall be disregarded when administering my estate".

If such contrary intention is not expressed in the Will then any advancement made to a child shall be brought into the reckoning of the administration of the estate and shall be taken as being so made in or towards satisfaction of the share of such child in the estate of the deceased.

63.—(1) Any advancement made to the child of a deceased person during his lifetime shall, subject to any contrary intention expressed or appearing from the circumstances of the case, be taken as being so made in or towards satisfaction of the share of such child in the estate of the deceased or the share which such child would have taken if living at the death of the deceased, and as between the children shall be brought into account in distributing the estate.

i. Residuary Clause. It is very important that every Will contains a residuary clause. The testator may feel that he has completely divided his assets and there is effectively nothing left. However matters can arise after his death. He may have come into certain monies or assets subsequent to the execution of the Will but prior to death. If the Will does not contain a residuary clause, then any balance of the property which has not been disposed of in accordance with the terms of the Will, will pass on intestacy and will be distributed in accordance with the rules of intestacy which may not be what the testator envisaged. It is very simple to include a residuary clause and for completeness all Wills should contain one. The following appropriate clause might be:

> "I give devise and bequeath the residue of my property of every nature and kind whatsoever and wheresoever situate to A and B in equal shares absolutely".

j. The Will must be dated.

k. The Will must be executed by the testator by signing clearly at the end of the Will.

l. The next paragraph is the attestation clause as follows:

> "Signed by the testator as and for his last will and testament in the presence of us both present at the same time who in his presence at his request and in the presence of each other have hereunder subscribed our names as attesting witnesses".

The witnesses should sign under the attestation clause and should include their address and description.

Witnesses

Certain persons should not witness a Will as follows:

1. In the case of a beneficiary or his spouse or a civil partner who witnesses a Will the devise or bequest made to that person fails. It should be noted that the attestation of the Will is not void but the gift to the witness is void.

2. A Solicitor executor who incorporates a charging clause in the Will loses his right to charge for the administration of the estate if he witnesses the Will.

Alterations of a Will Made After Execution

Alterations to a Will must be authenticated in accordance with s 86 of the Succession Act 1965:

> **86.**—An obliteration, interlineation, or other alteration made in a will after execution shall not be valid or have any effect, unless such alteration is executed as is required for the execution of the will; but the will, with such alteration as part thereof, shall be deemed to be duly executed if the signature of the testator and the signature of each witness is made in the margin or on some other part of the will opposite or near to such alteration, or at the foot or end of or opposite to a memorandum referring to such alteration, and written at the end of some other part of the will.

Instructions for a Will

A prudent solicitor should retain his instructions sheet. As a precautionary measure the instruction sheet should be kept with the Will, since these instructions are very helpful if there is a question as to the capacity of the testator at a later stage.

Storage of the Will

If the Will is to be stored in the solicitor's office, it should be recorded in a Wills register and in particular if the testator takes the original Will with him this should be noted by way of correspondence and a copy should be retained in the office with a note that the original was given to the testator after the execution of the Will.

This is very important particularly in cases where the original Will subsequently becomes lost. If it is shown that the original Will was lost in the Solicitor's office then the costs of an application for having a copy admitted to probate will have to be borne by the solicitor's office and not the estate.

Foreign Wills

A foreign Will may be regarded as a valid Will in Ireland even if it is not executed in accordance with s 78 of the Succession Act 1965.

Section 102 of the Succession Act 1965 states that a testamentary disposition shall be valid as regards form if the form complies with the internal law of

a. the place where it was made, or

b. the nationality possessed by the testator, or

c. the domicile possessed by the testator at the date of his Will or death,

d. the place where the testator had habitual residence, or in the case of immovables, the place where they are situate.

102.—(1) A testamentary disposition shall be valid as regards form if its form complies with the internal law –

(*a*) of the place where the testator made it, or

(*b*) of a nationality possessed by the testator, either at the time when he made the disposition, or at the time of his death, or

(*c*) of a place in which the testator had his domicile either at the time when he made the disposition, or at the time of his death, or

(*d*) of the place in which the testator had his habitual residence either at the time when he made the disposition, or at the time of his death, or

(*e*) so far as immovables are concerned, of the place where they are situated.

(2) Without prejudice to subsection (1), a testamentary disposition revoking an earlier testamentary disposition shall also be valid as regards form if it complies with any one of the laws according to the terms of which, under that subsection, the testamentary disposition that has been revoked was valid.

(3) For the purposes of this Part, if a national law consists of a non-unified system, the law to be applied shall be determined by the rules in force in that system and, failing any such rules, by the most real connexion which the testator had with any one of the various laws within that system.

(4) The determination of whether or not the testator had his domicile in a particular place shall be governed by the law of that place.

Two Wills

Probate may be granted in respect of two Wills if the following conditions are met:

1. They are not wholly inconsistent with each other and,

2. The later Will does not contain a revocation clause. However if there is an overlap of the dispositions then the later Will will be deemed to have revoked the earlier Will.

Testamentary Capacity

If the testator is an elderly person or if the Solicitor has some doubt as to the testamentary capacity of the testator then great care should be exercised in taking instructions and, if necessary, a medical opinion sought.

The test applied by the courts to determine testamentary capacity is a legal test as opposed to a medical test. The court will hold that the medical evidence of capacity is persuasive but it will not be fully decisive. The test applied by the court as to testamentary capacity of a testator is set out in *Banks v Goodfellow* (1870) LR5 QB 549 and this test was restated in the Supreme Court by Baron J in *Blackhall v Blackhall*, unreported, Supreme Court, 1 April 1998, as follows:

Sound testamentary capacity means that three things must exist at one and the same time:

1. The testator must understand that he is giving his property to one or more objects in his regard,

2. He must be able to recollect the extent of his property,

3. He must also understand the nature and extent of the claims upon him including those he is including in the Will and those he is excluding from the Will.

For the avoidance of doubt a prudent solicitor who has taken instructions for a Will from an elderly person should swear an affidavit of mental capacity bearing in mind the three matters in the test as outlined above.

Re the Goods of Glynn deceased, Glynn v Glynn (1990) 2 IR

Two doctors were of the opinion that the testator was disorientated on the day that he executed the Will and concluded that he was unable to communicate his own ideas. However, the evidence of the attesting witnesses was to the effect that they were both satisfied that the testator knew what he was doing and was capable at that point of making a Will. The Court was impressed by both of the attesting witnesses who had no private or personal interest in the estate of the deceased and despite the reservations of the doctors, the Court upheld the validity of the Will. Furthermore, a prudent solicitor will have the witnesses execute affidavits of attesting witness and these should be stored with the Will. This can obviate difficulty in the future if there is a question as to the attestation of the Will and the probate office require affidavits of attesting witness. Quite often there is a gap between the execution of the Will and the death of the testator and sometimes it is impossible to locate the attesting witnesses who may have been secretaries in the office at the time and who are now untraceable.

Duty of Care of Solicitor to the Legatees Named in the Will

The solicitor retained by the testator to attend to the drafting and execution of the will not only owes a duty of care to the testator to ensure that a valid will is created but also a duty of care to the beneficiaries named in the Will. Where it is established that a potential beneficiary under a will was deprived of that bequest by negligent drafting or failure to have the will executed in accordance with the provisions of the Succession Act the solicitor may be liable in damages to the disappointed beneficiary.

Wall v Hegarty [1980] 1 ILRM 124

The plaintiff, the executor named in a Will improperly attested and consequently ineffective, sought to recover damages from the defendants, a firm of solicitors retained by the testator to draft his will, for the loss of a legacy of £15,000 he would have received if the will had been operative and for the expense he had incurred in attempting to establish the will. The defendants admitted that the signature of the testator had not been duly authenticated by two witnesses and that the signature of one purported witness had been added subsequently in the solicitor's office. The plaintiff sought to establish that a solicitor owes a duty of care to the beneficiaries under a Will he is responsible for drafting.

Barrington J supported the plaintiff's claim and subsequently awarding him £16,350 and costs ruled:

(1) that a solicitor owes a duty of care to a legatee named in a draft Will to draft the Will with such reasonable care and skill as to ensure that the wishes of the testator are

not frustrated and the expectancy of the legatee defeated through lack of reasonable care and skill on his part:

(2) that the plaintiff's legal expenses in attempting to prove the invalid Will were recoverable under the principle in *Hedley Byrne & Co. Ltd. v Heller and Partners Ltd.* [1964] AC 465 because the defendants had failed to draw the plaintiff's attention to the irregularity that they knew to vitiate the will;

(3) that the plaintiff was entitled to damages under three heads following: loss of his legacy, the expense of proving the will, and interest to the abortive legacy as from the end of the executor's year.

Chapter 4

Court Application

Court applications involving probate matters may be divided in two: "contentious applications" and "non-contentious applications".

Non Contentious Probate Applications

Non contentious probate applications are made to the Probate Judge in the High Court, whereas a probate action (contentious applications) may be commenced in the High Court or the Circuit Court.

Order 50 of the Circuit Court Rules deals with probate matters and it refers to contentious probate actions. Order 79 of the Rules of the Superior Courts refers to non-contentious probate matters and deals with probate applications.

Probate Applications to Court

The following are the most common forms of applications made to the probate Judge:

A. Applications for a grant under s 27(4) of the Succession Act 1965 which includes the following:

   1. Application by a creditor for a creditor's grant.

   2. An application to bypass persons who have prior title.

B. Lost Wills where application is made to have a copy will admitted to probate.

C. Admitting a Will to proof by presumption as to due execution.

D. Where a cause of death recorded on the death certificate is something which may affect the capacity of the testator, Alzheimer's disease or dementia.

E. To set aside a caveat.

F. To apply for a grant *pendente lite* appointing an administrator *ad litem* for the purpose of proceedings.

G. To apply for a "Benjamin Order" where a beneficiary cannot be traced.

These applications are commenced by an originating Notice of Motion and grounding affidavit setting out the facts of the case being relied upon and sworn by the applicant.

Creditor's Grant

A creditor of the deceased, who is being frustrated in his attempts to recover from the estate of the deceased due to the failure of the persons entitled to extract probate or administration may make an application under s 27(4) for what has become known as a "Creditor's Grant" (see *Bank of Ireland v King* (1991) ILRM 796).

However, it would be necessary to cite the persons entitled to the grant before proceeding with an application under s 27(4).

By-Passing Persons with a Prior Title

If the person entitled to extract the grant is substantially delaying and failing to do so, an application by a beneficiary at the next level may be made under s 27(4). This could occur in the case of an unmarried person without issue who leaves a brother or sister and nephews and nieces who are the issue of the predeceased brother or sister. The living brothers or sisters are first entitled to extract the grant of administration but if they fail to do so, the nieces or nephews may make the application under s 27(4). This may also occur where any executor is failing to extract probate and has been cited and continues to fail to act. Then the person next entitled such as the universal legatee or residuary legatee may make the application.

Lost Wills

An application to permit a copy Will be admitted to probate where the original has been lost is also made in the non-contentious list. These are common applications and the three essential proofs are:

1. Proof that the Will was duly executed, by affidavits of due execution of the subscribing witnesses;

2. Proof that the original was in existence after the date of death of the testator.

3. Proof as to how the copy came into being and that it is authentic.

The notice parties to this application are the persons who would be affected by the making of the Order and in the case of a lost Will these will be the beneficiaries under a prior Will or the beneficiaries on intestacy whichever the case may be and consents should be obtained from these parties and such consents exhibited in the grounding affidavit.

Admitting a Will to Proof by Presumption of due Execution

This application Will be necessary when there is no attestation clause to a Will or if the attestation clause is insufficient and the Probate Officer is doubtful whether the will has been executed.

Essential proofs are:

1. Proof that the Will was duly executed by affidavits of due execution of the subscribing witnesses;

2. If subscribing witnesses are dead or affidavits cannot be obtained from them, then affidavits from:

    (a) Persons present at the execution of the will but who were not witnesses;

    (b) Evidence on affidavit of the fact of the handwriting of the deceased and the subscribing witnesses and also of any circumstances which may raise a presumption in favour of the due execution;

The notice parties to this application are the persons who would be affected by the making of the Order and in the case of a questionable will these will be the beneficiaries under a prior existing Will or the beneficiaries on intestacy whichever the case may be and consents should be obtained from these parties and such consents exhibited in the grounding affidavit.

Admitting a Will to Probate where a Cause of Death Recorded on the Death Certificate is Something which may Affect the Capacity of the Testator, Alzheimer's Disease or Dementia

Essential proofs are:

1. Proof that the Will was duly executed by affidavits of due execution by the subscribing witnesses who should aver to the mental capacity of the testator if possible;

2. Evidence on affidavit from the solicitor who took instructions from the testator, drafted the will and attended to its execution, that the testator was of sound mind and understanding and had testamentary capacity at the time of execution and if possible exhibiting instruction notes;

The notice parties to this application are the persons who would be affected by the making of the Order and in the case of a questionable will these will be the beneficiaries under a prior existing Will or the beneficiaries on intestacy whichever the case may be and consents should be obtained from these parties and such consents exhibited in the grounding affidavit.

To Set Aside a Caveat

The grounding affidavit should strongly question and attack the stated interest of the caveator.

To apply for a grant *pendente lite* appointing an administrator *ad litem* for purposes of proceedings

This application is necessary where the personal representatives of the proposed defendant have failed to apply for a grant and the applicant desires to commence proceedings which has subsisted against the estate of the deceased. Due to the time limit of two years for certain proceedings under s 9(2) of the Civil Liability Act 1961 these application are often last minute and rushed.

Proofs:

1. citation against the executor or possible administrator;

2. evidence on affidavit of proposed administrator *ad litem* (the applicant) consenting to act as administrator *ad litem* of the estate of the deceased for the purpose of the entitled intended action and that, if so appointed by the Court, will defend the said intended proceedings in the best interests of the estate of the said deceased and to the best of his ability and that he will represent the estate of the deceased in an independent and bona fide manner;

3. evidence on affidavit of the proposed plaintiff setting out the details of the proposed case exhibiting the deceased's death certificate and also a probate search showing that no grant has issued.

Benjamin Order

This is an order which is sought when a beneficiary in an estate cannot be located and the personal representative seeks liberty, without further enquiries, to administer and distribute the Estate of the said deceased on the footing that the missing beneficiary did not survive the said deceased and as if the said missing beneficiary was unmarried and without issue. The personal representative must carry out exhaustive searches and advertise and must lead this evidence on affidavit.

The order takes its name from the case of In *Re Benjamin Neville v Benjamin* [1902] 1 Ch 728.

Although it is a non contentious application the procedure differs from other non contentious probate applications in that it is commenced by Special Summons grounded on affidavit. When it come before the Master of the High Court it is transferred to the Judge's list and dealt with there.

The Circuit Court has jurisdiction to deal with this type of application due to the fact that it involves proceedings in respect of the administration of an estate of a deceased and any share therein. It is subject to the normal rules of jurisdiction of the Circuit Court as follows:

(a) That the deceased at the date of his death had a place of abode within the jurisdiction of the Court; and

(b) The value of the real estate comprised in the estate does not exceed €3,000,000.00 and does not have a rateable valuation exceeding €253.42.

Contentious Probate Applications

Contentious applications arise where someone wishes to challenge a Will or may consist of an application by the executor of a Will seeking to have the Will proved in solemn form. This can arise when there may be correspondence from a disaffected beneficiary who is indicating that they may challenge the Will or has indicated that the Will may not be valid but has not commenced proceedings. There are two ways in which a Will may be proved:

1. In solemn form.
2. In common form.

Solemn Form

A Will is said to be proved in solemn form when, after a Court hearing, the Judge pronounces in favour of the Will and declares the Will to be proved in solemn form.

Once this happens and no Appeal is lodged against the Judge's decision, the Will is then unchallengeable after that. When a Will have been proved in solemn form and is admitted to Probate, that Probate is unquestionable and cannot be challenged.

Common Form

A Will is proved in common form when it is admitted to Probate in the normal course. When the Grant of Probate issues from the Probate Office or the District Probate Registry, the Will is proved and that is known as proof in common form. However, this grant can be challenged at a later stage. If the person who seeks to challenge it is within time they may seek to have the Will challenged and have the probate revoked.

Probate Actions

A Probate action is where proceedings are issued seeking one of the following:

A. Challenging the Will (seeking to condemn the will) or

B. To revoke a Grant of Representation (either probate or administration).

Effectively both actions amount to the same thing and the proceedings for having a Grant of Representation revoked will always have their origins in the fact that the Plaintiff seeks to challenge the Will and have it condemned. If the grant has issued the proceedings will seek to have the Grant of Probate revoked and the will condemned.

In the case of an intestacy it may be that someone is seeking to have the Grant of Administration revoked on the grounds that it was granted to an incorrect person. If somebody who claims to have a superior entitlement to the grant turns up, they may seek to have the original administration revoked and administration granted to them instead.

Grounds for Challenging a Will

The usual grounds for challenging a Will are the three statutory pleas which effectively are an amalgam of ss 77 and 78 of the Succession Act 1965 and are as follows:

1. The Will was not executed in accordance with the terms of the Succession Act 1965,

2. The testator was not of sound deposing mind and

3. The testator did not know and approve of the contents of the Will.

Other pleas which may be included are:

4. The testator was unduly influenced in or about the making of the Will.

5. Execution of the Will was obtained by fraud.

The latter two pleas should not be made lightly and should only be included in the proceedings where there is strong and stateable evidence available. The Rules of the Superior Courts require specifically that in all cases alleging misrepresentation, fraud, breach of trust, wilful default or undue influence that particulars (with dates) that shall be set out in the pleadings.

> "Order 19 Rule 5(2)) In all cases alleging misrepresentation, fraud, breach of trust, wilful default or undue influence and in all other cases in which particulars may be necessary, particulars (with dates and items if necessary) shall be set out in the pleadings."

There is a danger that if a bald assertion of undue influence or fraud is made in the pleadings without any particulars including dates and names of persons, the proceedings may be struck out for lack of particulars.

There is also a substantial danger that costs will be awarded against an unsuccessful plaintiff who has pleaded fraud. The question of costs is a matter of discretion vested in the Trial Judge and if the plaintiff makes out a good stateable case in relation to other matters other than fraud, but yet fails to succeed in the case, he still may be awarded his costs out of the estate. Costs will certainly be awarded if he succeeds.

In relation to cases based on fraud or undue influence, the third party who, it is alleged, exercised the undue influence or perpetrated the fraud, should be joined in the proceedings as defendants.

Other contentious matters would be as follows:

1. Applications under s 117 of the Succession Act 1965 by a child of the testator.

2. Proceedings against the executor or administrator to administer the estate. It should be noted that in the latter case such proceedings cannot be brought without leave of the Court before the expiration of one year from the date of the death of the deceased. The only exception to this is where creditors of a deceased person are bringing proceedings against the personal representatives. This is in accordance with s 62 of the Succession Act 1965.

62.—(1) The personal representatives of a deceased person shall distribute his estate as soon after his death as is reasonably practicable having regard to the nature of the estate, the manner in which it is required to be distributed and all other relevant circumstances, but proceedings against the personal representatives in respect of their failure to distribute shall not, without leave of the court, be brought before the expiration of one year from the date of the death of the deceased.

(2) Nothing in this section shall prejudice or affect the rights of creditors of a deceased person to bring proceedings against his personal representatives before the expiration of one year from his death.

3. Other contentious proceedings might be proceedings against the personal representatives to distribute the estate in accordance with the Succession Act 1965. Sometimes personal representatives fail to take into account advancements made to children of the testator pursuant to s 63. See chapter 3.

Probate Actions Procedure

Procedure for Probate Actions in the High Court

A Probate action in the High Court is defined in Order 25, Rule 1 of the RSC as follows:

> "Probate Action" means any proceeding commenced by originating summons and seeking the grant or recall of Probate, Letters of Administration or similar relief".

The procedure for Probate actions is as follows:

1. If the Grant has not issued, a caveat must be entered in the Probate Office.

2. A Plenary Summons should be issued from the Central Office and the Indorsement has to show whether the Plaintiff claims as creditor, executor, administrator,

residuary legatee, legatee, next of kin, heir at law, devisee or in any or what other capacity – *Order 4, Rule 10 RSC.*

3. Before the Summons in Probate proceedings can be issued the plaintiff must file an Affidavit of Verification of the Indorsement on the Summons and on the issuing of the Summons, the plaintiff shall, if he has not already done so, lodge a caveat in the Probate Office entitled in the estate of the deceased person.

4. An Affidavit of Scripts by the plaintiff and the defendant must be filed within eight days of the Entry of Appearance on the part of the defendant whether the parties have or have not any scripts in their possession – *Order 12, Rule 27 RSC.*

5. After the closing of the pleadings, the plaintiff must apply by Notice of Motion to the Master for directions to fix the time and mode of trial.

The above is the procedure in the High Court of a Probate action as defined by Order 125 and it should be noted that the Probate action is any proceeding seeking the grant or recall of Probate or Letters of Administration or similar relief.

Certain other matters can arise which do not fall within the definition of Probate actions which are matters of contention between the parties and these matters are commenced by the issue of a Special Summons and are set out in Order 3, Rules RR(1)–(8) RSC, as follows:

(1) The administration of the real or personal estate of a deceased person, or the administration of the trust of any deed or instrument save where there is a charge of wilful default or breach of trust.

(2) The determination of any question affecting the rights or interests of any person claiming to be creditor, devisee, legatee, next-of-kin or heir-at-law of a deceased person, or *cestui que trust* under the trust of any deed or instrument, or claiming by assignment or otherwise under any such person.

(3) The payment into Court of any money in the hands of executors, administrators or trustees.

(4) A direction to any executors, or administrators or trustees to do or abstain from doing any particular act in their character as such executors or administrators or trustees (including the furnishing and vouching of accounts).

(5) The approval of any sale, purchase, compromise, or other transaction in connection with the administration of any estate or trust.

(6) The determination of any question arising in the administration of any estate or trust or the ascertainment of any class of creditors, legatees, devisees, next-of-kin, or others.

(7) The determination of any question of construction arising under any deed, will, or other written instrument, and a declaration of the rights of the persons interested.

(8) The determination, under the Finance Act, 1894, s 14 (2), of a dispute as to the proportion of estate duty to be borne by any property or person.

As will be seen the questions to be answered by Special Summons are wide ranging and in particular number two is fairly all encompassing.

Generally the applications which are brought by way of Special Summons include the following:

1. Where a beneficiary is dissatisfied with the administration of the Estate.

2. Where there is a question to be determined affecting the rights or interests of a person claiming to be entitled to the Estate whether as a legatee or creditor.

3. The determination of any question arising in relation to the ascertainment of any class of creditors, legatees, devisees, next of kin or others.

4. Any question in relation to the construction of any Deed, Will or other written instrument.

5. Applications under s 117 of the Succession Act 1965.

6. Any question in relation to the legal right share of the spouse.

7. Any question in relation to appropriation by the Personal Representative or by the surviving spouse in relation to the dwellinghouse.

Procedure for Probate Actions in the Circuit Court

The procedure in the Circuit Court is similar to the High Court and is regulated by Order 50 of the Rules of the Circuit Court 2001:

1. Lodge a caveat in the Probate Office entitled in the Estate of the deceased.

2. Obtain a certificate of rateability valuation of the real estate.

3. Issue a Civil Bill which is headed Testamentary Civil Bill.

4. Complete a Verifying Affidavit as in the High Court.

5. Complete an Affidavit of Scripts, whether the party has any scripts in its possession or not. The Affidavit of Scripts to be filed within ten days of the Entry of Appearance.

A Testamentary Civil Bill is used in proceedings issued for the purpose of obtaining a grant or revocation of a Grant of Probate or Letters of Administration. Any other proceedings in relation to the Estate or administration of the Estate, pursuant to the Succession Act 1965, are commenced by a Succession Law Civil Bill. The procedure in relation to pleadings whether a Testamentary Civil Bill or a Succession Act Civil Bill is very similar. In both cases a caveat must be lodged in the Probate Office entitled in the Estate of the deceased person.

Costs in Probate Actions

The law in relation to costs in relation to Probate actions was restated by the Supreme Court in *Elliott v Stamp* [2009] 3 IR 387.

In that case the defendants were the principal beneficiaries of the Will of the deceased. The plaintiff pleaded in the Statement of Claim that the deceased had lacked testamentary capacity and that the Will was procured by the duress or undue influence of either or both of the defendants. Prior to the hearing of the matter before the High Court, the plaintiff withdrew the claim in relation to testamentary capacity and proceeded on the claim of undue influence alone. The High Court upheld the Will, finding the deceased to have been of sound mind and finding no undue influence or duress on the part of the defendant, but awarded the plaintiff one third of her costs to be paid out of the deceased's Estate.

On Appeal to the Supreme Court on the issue of costs, the plaintiff argued that the High Court had erred in law in failing to order that full costs be paid out of the deceased's Estate. It was submitted by the defendants that the Court had discretion not to award costs to an unsuccessful plaintiff when an Executor has disclosed all relevant information to that plaintiff prior to hearing. Held by the Supreme Court in allowing the Appeal:

1. That, following an action challenging the validity of a Will the Court had a discretion to award an unsuccessful plaintiff her full costs out of the Estate of the deceased, provided that there were reasonable grounds for the litigation and provided the action was conducted bona fide.

2. That, should the Judge decide to award only partial costs to an unsuccessful plaintiff in such matters, the basis for such decision should be clearly stated.

This case applied the principles of an earlier case *In Bonis Morelli: Vella v Morelli* [1968] IR 11.

It appears therefore that if the unsuccessful plaintiff had reasonable grounds for the litigation and conducted the case bona fide then that plaintiff, although unsuccessful in the proceedings, would be awarded the costs.

The Judge (Kearns J) went on to state obiter that it was preferable where possible for a defendant to an action challenging the validity of a Will, to disclose all relevant documentation in advance upon which he intends to rely at the trial of the matter so that claims that might no longer be made in light of such disclosure might be reconsidered and withdrawn, if necessary.

(34) "I believe the defendants in this case were entirely correct to set out by means of statements and reports the evidence which they proposed to rely on at trial. I would encourage such an initiative in all testamentary proceedings which lend themselves to such steps. It is beyond doubt that small Estates can be entirely dissipated by legal proceedings brought by disappointed parties whose intention may be to force the Executor into some form of settlement or vindictively to waste the assets in legal proceedings which, even if capable of being seen as properly brought at the onset, can no longer be seen as such once the full picture has been made available by those defending the proceedings. I see this as the equivalent in Probate terms of a lodgement or tender made in personal injuries actions. I believe it is an approach which should be adopted whenever possible. It would represent a valuable protection for the Estates of deceased persons, without in any way diluting the principles enunciated in *Bonis Morelli: Vella v. Morelli* [1968] IR11. Thus while it may be reasonable to commence and bring proceedings, and to bring them bona fide, a point

may arrive where, as a result of disclosure made by the defence, the future maintenance of the claim can no longer be seen as reasonable".

Chapter 5

Section 117 of the Succession Act 1965

Introduction

Proceedings may be brought by a child of a testator who feels that s/he was unfairly treated by his/her parent under the terms of the Will. The proceedings are brought pursuant to s 117 of the Succession Act 1965.

117.—(1) Where, on application by or on behalf of a child of a testator, the court is of opinion that the testator has failed in his moral duty to make proper provision for the child in accordance with his means, whether by his will or otherwise, the court may order that such provision shall be made for the child out of the estate as the court thinks just.

(1A) *(a)* An application made under this section by virtue of *Part V* of the Status of Children Act, 1987, shall be considered in accordance with subsection (2) irrespective of whether the testator executed his will before or after the commencement of the said *Part V*.

(b) Nothing in paragraph *(a)* shall be construed as conferring a right to apply under this section in

respect of a testator who dies before the commencement of the said *Part V*.

NOTE: Subsection 1A inserted by Status of Children Act 1987, s 31.

(2) The court shall consider the application from the point of view of a prudent and just parent, taking into account the position of each of the children of the testator and any other circumstances which the court may consider of assistance in arriving at a decision that will be as fair as possible to the child to whom the application relates and to the other children.

(3) An order under this section shall not affect the legal right of a surviving spouse or, if the surviving spouse is the mother or father of the child, any devise or bequest to the spouse or any share to which the spouse is entitled on intestacy.

(3A) An order under this section shall not affect the legal right of a surviving civil partner unless the court, after consideration of all the circumstances, including the testator's financial circumstances and his or her obligations to the surviving civil partner, is of the opinion that it would be unjust not to make the order.

NOTE: Subsection 3A inserted by The Civil Partnership and Certain Rights and Obligations Cohabitants Act 2010, s 86.

(4) Rules, of court shall provide for the conduct of proceedings under this section in a summary manner.

(5) The costs in the proceedings shall be at the discretion of the court.

(6) An order under this section shall not be made except on an application made within [six] months from the first taking out of representation of the deceased's estate.

NOTE: s 117(6) amended by s 46 of the Family Law (Divorce) Act 1996.

Rights conferred under s 117 are not absolute rights but merely permit the child to make application to the court for the court to consider whether the parent acted as a just and prudent parent in distributing his or her estate and in dealing with the child. If the child can prove that the parent failed in his/her moral duty either by Will or during his/her lifetime to make proper provision for the child in accordance with his/her means, the court is then empowered to make proper provision for the child out of the estate in a manner of a just and prudent parent.

The following matters should be noted in relation to s 117:

1. In a case where a spouse leaves the whole of his estate to the remaining spouse who is the mother or father of the child then the child will not have a cause of action due to the fact that any order made under the section shall not affect any devise or bequest to that spouse or any share to which the spouse is entitled on intestacy. See s 117(3).

2. However, if the estate was divided in such a way that the surviving spouse was left two thirds of the estate and a portion of the estate devised to some third party, including a sibling of the child, the child may then maintain an action under s 117.

3. In a case where the surviving spouse is not the mother or father of the child, the child may commence proceedings against the estate but the legal right share of that surviving spouse will not be affected by such proceedings.

4. In the case of a civil partner, the legal right share of the civil partner does not enjoy the same protection as the legal right share of a spouse. Depending on the circumstances of the case, the court in these proceedings after considering all the circumstances of the case may reduce the legal right share (s 117(3A)).

The courts have, since 1967, developed jurisprudence in dealing with cases under s 117 and the most recent restatement of the criteria to be examined was set out by Mr Justice Kearns

In the Estate of ABC deceased, XC, YC and ZC v RT, KU & JL (2003) 2 IR 250:

(a) The social policy underlying s 117 is primarily directed to protecting those children who are still where they might reasonably expect support from their parents, against the failure of parents who are unmindful of their duties in that area.

(b) What has to be determined is whether the testator, at the time of his death, owes any moral obligation to the children and if so, whether he has failed in that obligation.

(c) There is a high onus of proof placed on an applicant for relief under s 117, which requires the establishment of a positive failure in moral duty.

(d) Before a court can interfere, there must be clear circumstances and a positive failure in moral duty must be established.

(e) The duty created by s 117 is not absolute.

(f) The relationship of parent and child does not, itself and without regard to other circumstances, create a moral duty to leave anything by will to the child.

(g) Section 117 does not create an obligation to leave something to each child.

(h) The provision of an expensive education for a child may discharge, the moral duty as may other gifts or settlements made during the lifetime of the testator.

(i) Financing a good education so as to give a child the best start in life possible and providing money, which, if properly managed, should afford a degree of financial security for the rest of one's life, does amount to making "proper provision".

(j) The duty under s 117 is not to make adequate provision but to provide proper provision in accordance with the testator's means.

(k) A just parent must take into account not just his moral obligations to his children and to his wife, but all his moral obligations, e.g. to aged and infirm parents.

(l) In dealing with a s 117 application, the position of an applicant child is not to be taken in isolation. The court's duty is to consider the entirety of the testator's affairs and to decide upon the application in the overall context. In other words, while the moral claim of a child may require a testator to make a particular provision for him, the moral claims of others may require such provision to be reduced or omitted altogether.

(m) Special circumstances giving rise to a moral duty may arise if a child is induced to believe that by, for example, working on a farm, he will ultimately become the owner of it, thereby causing him to shape his upbringing, training and life accordingly.

(n) Another example of special circumstances might be a child who had a long illness or an exceptional talent which it would be morally wrong not to foster.

(o) Special needs would also include physical or mental disability.

(p) Although the court has very wide powers both as to when to make provision for an applicant child and as to the nature of such provision, such powers must not be construed as giving the court a power to make a new will for the testator.

(q) The test to be applied is not which of the alternative courses open to the testator the court itself would have adopted if confronted with the same situation but, rather, whether the decision of the testator to opt for the course he did, of itself and without more, constituted a breach of moral duty to the plaintiff.

(r) The court must not disregard the fact that parents must be presumed to know their children better than anyone else.

It is very difficult to give a definitive answer in any individual case as to whether a court will grant relief under s 117. Each case will stand on its own merits and the relationship between the testator and the child and the financial circumstances of the child will all be taken into consideration.

When advising a client in relation to the possibility of bringing s 117 proceedings instructions should be taken on the following matters:

(a) the income of the testator;

(b) the total value of the estate;

(c) the income of each of the plaintiffs and spouses;

(d) the total value of the assets of each of the plaintiffs and spouses;

(e) the education the plaintiffs received and was it provided by the testator;

(f) any gifts given by the testator during his/her lifetime;

(g) the relationship of each of the plaintiffs with the testator, this would include how often they would visit him/her, did any of them provide for him/her, taking them out, providing meals, etc.;

(h) details of any promises made by the testator to the plaintiffs promising property or any of the assets;

(i) each of them should state why they feel that the testator failed in his/her moral duty to provide;

(j) Any special circumstances giving rise to a moral duty, was the child induced to stay at home and provide for the testator on the foot of a promise of property.

Time Limits

The time limit for bringing an application under s 117 is very short and is six months from the date of taking out representation of the deceased's estate pursuant to the Succession Act 1965, s 117 (6) amended by the Family Law (Divorce) Act 1996, s 46.

A solicitor who is consulted by a child should ideally lodge a caveat in the Probate Office since that will bring the intention of the child to the notice of the solicitors acting for the estate. The solicitor acting for the child will have to be very vigilant to ascertain when representation was first granted. It is advisable to have the proceedings drafted by Counsel and ready to be issued and served once the grant issues.

The proceedings under s 117 may be brought in the High Court or the Circuit Court depending on the value of the real estate comprised in the estate and the usual place of abode of the testator at the date of death.

Proceedings under s 117 shall be heard in Chambers pursuant to s 119 of the Succession Act 1965.

119.—All proceedings in relation to this Part shall be heard in chambers.

Chapter 6

Legal Right Share

A legal right share is the automatic share which is conferred on a spouse or civil partner of a testator as set out in s 111 and s 111A of the Succession Act 1965.

> 111.—(1) If the testator leaves a spouse and no children, the spouse shall have a right to one-half of the estate.
>
> (2) If the testator leaves a spouse and children, the spouse shall have a right to one-third of the estate.
>
> 111A.—(1) If the testator leaves a civil partner and no children, the civil partner shall have a right to one-half of the estate.
>
> (2) Subject to section 117(3A), if the testator leaves a civil partner and children, the civil partner shall have a right to one-third of the estate.
>
> NOTE: s 111A inserted by the Civil Partnership and Certain Rights and Obligations Cohabitants Act 2010, s 81.

The legal right share takes priority over devises, bequests and shares on intestacy.

112.—The right of a spouse under section 111 or the right of a civil partner under section 111A (which shall be known as a legal right) shall have priority over devises, bequests and shares on intestacy.

NOTE: s 112 amended by the Civil Partnership and Certain Rights and Obligations Cohabitants Act 2010, s 79.

However, the legal right share in favour of a civil partner does not enjoy the same automatic priority as the legal right share in favour of a spouse. Depending on the circumstances of the case, the court in s 117 proceedings (see chapter 5) after considering all the circumstances of the case may reduce the legal right share.

117(3A).—An order under this section shall not affect the legal right of a surviving civil partner unless the court, after consideration of all the circumstances, including the testator's financial circumstances and his or her obligations to the surviving civil partner, is of the opinion that it would be unjust not to make the order.

NOTE: Succession Act 1965, s 117(3A) inserted by the Civil Partnership and Certain Rights and Obligations Cohabitants Act 2010, s 86.

Renunciation of Legal Right Share

The legal right may be renounced in a written ante nuptial contract or in the case of a civil partner an ante civil partnership registration contract.

113.—The legal right of a spouse may be renounced in an ante-nuptial contract made in writing between the parties to an intended marriage or may be renounced in writing by the spouse after marriage and during the lifetime of the testator.

113A.—The legal right of a civil partner may be renounced in an ante-civil-partnership-registration contract made in writing between the parties to an intended civil partnership or may be renounced in writing by the civil partner after registration and during the lifetime of the testator."

NOTE: s 113A inserted by the Civil Partnership and Certain Rights and Obligations Cohabitants Act 2010, s 83.

The legal right is conferred on surviving spouses and civil partners except in that case it is subject to the provisions of s 117(3A) of the Succession Act 1965.

Nature of the Right

There was some uncertainty as to the nature of the legal right share as to whether it was an automatic right or a right exercisable by the surviving spouse until the Supreme Court decision in *O'Dwyer v Keegan* [1997] 2 IR 585.

In that matter a testator died without making provision in his Will for his wife. She died 12 hours after the testator without regaining consciousness. There were no children of the marriage and the wife had never renounced her legal right share and she was not precluded by s 120 of the Succession Act from taking her share in the spouse's estate.

It was held by the Supreme Court (Murphy, Lynch and Barron, JJ):

1. That a surviving spouse had a legal right pursuant to s 111(1) to a share in the estate of his or her deceased spouse. This right has the same quality as an interest arising under a Will or a share arising on an intestacy and, similarly, arose on the death of the testator.

2. That it was necessary to consider the meaning to be given to the words "shall have a right to" rather than merely the word "right" in the context in which it was used in the sub-section.

3. That, furthermore, in the absence of any procedure whereby a surviving spouse could be notified of the right conferred by the sub-section and given the opportunity to exercise, it was fatal to the contention that the right was one which was exercisable only at the option of the surviving spouse.

Therefore, it appears that the legal right share vests in the surviving spouse without requiring any action on the part of that surviving spouse to ensure such vesting.

This has to be distinguished from s 115 of the Act whereby a surviving spouse has a right to elect between a bequest arising under a Will or the legal right share arising under s 111.

Where the testator does not make any provision in the Will for the spouse, on the testator's death the legal right share then automatically vests in the spouse. By contrast, where the testator makes a bequest to the spouse under the terms of the Will the spouse must then elect between the bequest under the Will or opt for the legal right share. This is a right which is exercisable at the option of the surviving spouse and this right is granted under s 115 of the Act so when there is a bequest to the spouse the legal right share does not automatically vest in the spouse and only vests if the spouse elects to take same.

This was held by the Supreme Court *In the matter of the Estate of Douglas D Urquhart, deceased; The Revenue Commissioners v Allied Irish Banks* [1974] 1 IR 197.

Section 1 of the Finance Act 1894, provides that estate duty shall be paid on the value of property which passes on the death of a deceased, including property of which the deceased at the time of his death was "competent to dispose". Section 22(2)(*a*), of the Act of 1894 provides that a person shall be deemed competent to dispose of property if he has such an estate or interest therein or such "general power" as would enable him to dispose of the property, including "every power or authority enabling the donee or other holder thereof to appoint or dispose of property as he thinks fit".

Section 111 of the Succession Act 1965, provides that, if a testatrix leaves a spouse and no children, the spouse shall have a right to one-half of the estate of the testatrix; and s 112 states that such right shall be known as a "legal right." Section 115(1) of the Act of 1965 provides that, where under the will of a deceased who dies wholly testate, there is a devise or bequest to a spouse, the spouse "may elect to take either that devise or bequest or the share to which he is entitled as a legal right" and that, in default of election, the spouse shall be entitled to take under the will only.

In this case a wife died, having bequeathed by her Will a legacy to her husband on condition that he should survive her for a month. She was not survived by any children of her marriage. Her husband survived her by one day and then died without having made an election pursuant to s 115 of the Act of 1965, so that the husband's estate was not benefited by a legal right or by the legacy. In these circumstances the plaintiffs claimed that a half share in his wife's estate was property of which the husband was competent to dispose at the time of his death for the purposes of the Finance Act, 1894. On appeal by the executors of the will of the husband from a decision of the High Court in favour of the claim, it was

Held by the Supreme Court (FitzGerald CJ, Walsh and Henchy JJ), in allowing the appeal:

1. That, in order to establish the plaintiffs' claim, it was necessary to establish that the husband at the date of his death had power to dispose of a statutory one-half share in his wife's estate.

2. That, as the wife had died wholly testate leaving her husband but no children, the husband had a statutory right to elect to take either a statutory one-half share in the wife's estate or the share bequeathed to him in her will.

3. (Henchy J dissenting) that, as he had not elected to take a statutory one-half share in his wife's estate, the husband at the time of his death had no power to dispose of such statutory share.

Right of Election Regarding Legal Right Share

Where there is a devise or bequest to a spouse or civil partner under a Will, the spouse or civil partner has a right to elect to take either the devise or bequest or the legal right share.

The time limit for election is either six months from the date of receipt by the spouse of a notice of election served by the personal representatives or one year from the date of the grant of representation, whichever is the later.

In default of election the spouse of a civil partner shall not be entitled to take the legal right share.

Where the spouse or civil partner is a person of unsound mind the right of election may be exercised by the spouse's or civil partner's committee or, if no committee, by the appropriate Court.

115.—(1)(a)Where, under the will of a deceased person who dies wholly testate, there is a devise or bequest to a spouse or civil partner, the spouse or civil partner may elect to take either that devise or bequest or the share to which he is entitled as a legal right.

(b) In default of election, the spouse or civil partner shall be entitled to take under the will, and he shall not be entitled to take any share as a legal right.

(2)(a) Where a person dies partly testate and partly intestate, a spouse or civil partner may elect to take either –

(i) his share as a legal right, or

(ii) his share under the intestacy, together with any devise or bequest to him under the will of the deceased.

(*b*) In default of election, the spouse or civil partner shall be entitled to take his share under the intestacy, together with any devise or bequest to him under the will, and he shall not be entitled to take any share as a legal right.

(3) A spouse or civil partner, in electing to take his share as a legal right, may further elect to take any devise or bequest to him less in value than the share in partial satisfaction thereof.

(4) It shall be the duty of the personal representatives to notify the spouse or civil partner in writing of the right of election conferred by this section. The right shall not be exercisable after the expiration of six months from the receipt by the spouse or civil partner of such notification or one year from the first taking out of representation of the deceased's estate, whichever is the later.

(5) Where the surviving spouse or civil partner is a person of unsound mind, the right of election conferred by this section may, if there is a committee of the spouse's or civil partner's estate, be exercised on behalf of the spouse or civil partner by the committee by leave

of the court which has appointed the committee or, if there is no committee, be exercised by the High Court or, in a case within the jurisdiction of the Circuit Court, by that Court.

(6) In this section, but only in its application to a case to which subsection (1) of section 114 applies, "devise or bequest" means a gift deemed under that subsection to have been made by the will of the testator.

NOTE: s 115 amended by the Civil Partnership and Certain Rights and Obligations Cohabitants Act 2010, s 85 (a) and (b).

If a spouse dies before an election is made, the legal right share does not form part of the spouse's estate: *Reilly v McEntee* (1984) ILRM 572.

Chapter 7

Time Limits in Probate Matters

Introduction

Our law has long recognised that there has to be a limit on the time in which proceedings may be taken or certain acts done and there has been a policy of ensuring efficiencies in the administration of justice by setting time limits in which certain steps must be taken or proceedings issued. This is illustrated by the Statute of Limitations Act 1957 and the subsequent amending legislation to that Act. In probate matters the statutory limitations on the length of time in which certain acts must be done promotes greater efficiencies in the administration of estates. Practitioners should be aware of all time restraints in relation to legal proceedings and probate matters are no exception. In dealing with probate matters the limits which apply to the estates of deceased persons and various procedural matters are contained in the Succession Act and other enactments.

This chapter is to give an overview of the most regular general time limits which apply in relation to estates of deceased persons and also the various time limits which arise under certain aspects of the Succession Act.

Actions Subsisting Against the Estate of a Deceased Person at Date of Death

Two Years or Less from the Date of Death

The time limit for commencing proceedings against the estate of a deceased person in respect of an action which has survived against the estate is two years from the date of death or less.

9.—(1) In this section "the relevant period" means the period of limitation prescribed by the Statute of Limitations or any other limitation enactment.

(2) No proceedings shall be maintainable in respect of any cause of action whatsoever which has survived against the estate of a deceased person unless either –

(*a*) proceedings against him in respect of that cause of action were commenced within the relevant period and were pending at the date of his death, or

(*b*) proceedings are commenced in respect of that cause of action within the relevant period or within the period of two years after his death, whichever period first expires.

NOTE: Civil Liability Act 1961, s 9

Section 9 refers to proceedings in relation to causes of action which have survived against the estate of a deceased person and it also refers to the relevant period. The time starts to run from the date the cause of action arises.

Section 9(1)(b) states that the proceedings must be commenced in respect of the cause of action within the relevant period or within a period of two years after his death, whichever period first expires.

By way of illustration, if X has a cause of action against Y on a simple contract, the period of limitation is six years. If X delays to commence proceedings for a period of three years then, in the normal course of events, X still has three years in which to commence the proceedings before the cause of action is statute barred. However, if Y dies after three years, the remaining period is reduced to two years subsequent to the date of death since that period will first expire.

It should be noted that this limit is in respect of actions which have survived against the estate of a deceased person. The type of action envisaged by this section is where there may be outstanding claims against the estate in tort or contract or claims relating to property. Personal representatives sometimes use this time limit to their advantage by neglecting to raise representation to the estate for more than a period of two years in order to frustrate the bringing of proceedings. In these circumstances the potential plaintiff should make an application to a court to appoint an "administrator *ad Litem*" for the purposes of defending the action (see page 50). Proceedings may be served on such administrator within the time limit of two years.

It appears, however, that for s 9 of the Civil Liability Act 1961 to apply, the cause of action must be subsisting at the date of death and unless it was subsisting at the date of death the normal period in the statute of limitations will apply instead of the two year period under s 9(2).

The Governor and Company of Bank of Ireland v Kathleen O'Keeffe [1987] 1 IR 48

On the 19 February 1985 proceedings were instituted against the defendant as legal personal representative of MO'K, who died on the 11 February 1982, for monies due on foot of a continuing guarantee dated the 18 November 1980 whereby MO'K had guaranteed to pay, on demand, the debts of B Ltd. A demand for payment on foot of the guarantee had not been made against his estate until the 6 May 1982.

The defendant disputed the plaintiff's claim by arguing that it was statute barred in that the proceedings were commenced more than two years after the date of death by virtue of s 9(2) of the Civil Liability Act 1961. The matter was heard in the High Court by Baron J who gave judgment in favour of the plaintiffs on the basis:

1. That the plaintiff's cause of action on foot of the guarantee did not arise until after the demand was made;

2. That since the plaintiff's demand had not been made until after the death of the deceased, there was no cause of action subsisting against him at the time of his death and, accordingly, s 9(2) of the 1961 Act was not applicable.

> The claim which is brought is one which is not maintainable until after a demand made and no cause of action could have arisen until such demand was made – see *Re: J Brown's Estate, Brown v Brown* [1893] 2 Ch 300.

In that case [*Brown*] there was a joint and several covenant in a mortgage by the deceased and his son to pay the principal on demand and in the meantime to pay interest. The deceased joined in the mortgage as a surety only. Several years after his death demand was made against his Estate on foot of the covenant. It was held that no cause of action had accrued against his Estate until such demand. It seems to me that similarly in the present case no cause of action existed whereby the Plaintiff could sue either the deceased or his Estate until demand had been made. Since this demand was not made until after the death of the deceased, it follows that there was no cause of action subsisting against him at the date of his death. Accordingly the Defence fails". Per Barron J at 49.

Action to Establish and/or Enforce Entitlement to an Estate

Six Years from Date of Death

Proceedings to establish and/or enforce an entitlement to a share in the estate of a deceased person must be commenced within a period six years from the date when the right to receive the share or interest accrued. This is generally the date of death. This is not an action which has survived against the Estate of a deceased person but only arises on the death of the deceased and the limitation is clearly set out in the Succession Act, s 126.

126.–The Statute of Limitations, 1957, is hereby amended by the substitution of the following section for section 45:

45. (1) Subject to section 71, no action in respect of any claim to the estate of a deceased person or to any share or interest in such estate, whether under a will, on intestacy or under section 111 or section 111A of the Succession Act, 1965, shall be brought after the

expiration of six years from the date when the right to receive the share or interest accrued.

(2) No action to recover arrears of interest in respect of any legacy or damages in respect of such arrears shall be brought after the expiration of three years from the date on which the interest became due.

NOTE: Statute Of Limitations 1957, s 45 substituted by s 126 of the Succession Act 1965 and amended by s 86 of the Civil Partnership and Certain Rights and Obligations Cohabitants Act 2010.

Election by Spouse between Legal Right Share and Bequest Under Will

Six months after receipt of notification from personal representative or one year from the first taking out of the grant of representation:

It is the duty of the personal representatives to notify the spouse or civil partner in writing of the right of election. The section is unclear as to what happens if the personal representatives fail in their duty to notify the spouse or civil partner but note that the right is not exercisable after the expiration of six months from the receipt by the spouse or civil partner of such notification or one year from the first taking out of representation of the deceased's estate, whichever is the later.

Therefore it would appear that if the personal representatives fail to serve a Notice of Election on the spouse or civil partner then the later time limit of one year from the taking out of representation will apply and must be adhered to.

Practitioners advising a spouse or civil partner in this situation should ensure that the spouse or civil partner elects within the relevant period of one year and should not wait for the personal representatives to serve a Notice of Election on the spouse or civil partner. If the spouse or civil partner wishes to elect for the legal right share as opposed to the bequest under the Will, then it is best to make a pre-emptive move and serve the election on the personal representatives even before they serve a Notice of Election on the spouse or civil partner.

It shall be the duty of the personal representatives to notify the spouse or civil partner in writing of the right of election conferred by this section. The right shall not be exercisable after the expiration of six months from the receipt by the spouse of such notification or one year from the first taking out of representation of the deceased's estate, whichever is the later.

NOTE: Succession Act 1965, s 115(4) as amended by the Civil Partnership and Certain Rights and Obligations of Cohabitants Act 2010, s 85. See *Reilly v McEntee* (1984) ILRM 572 if the spouse wishes to acquire the legal right share.

Exercise of right of Spouse or Civil Partner to have the dwelling appropriated

Six months after receipt of notification of the right from personal representative or one year from the first taking out of the grant of representation.

It is the duty of the personal representatives to notify the spouse or civil partner in writing of the right to have the dwelling appropriated to him/her. The section is unclear as to what happens if the personal representatives fail in their duty to notify the spouse or civil partner and the right is not exercisable after the expiration of six months from the receipt by the spouse or civil partner of such notification or one year from the first taking out of representation of the deceased's estate whichever is the later.

Therefore it would appear that if the personal representatives fail to serve a Notice of Election on the spouse or civil partner then the later time limit of one year from the taking out of representation will apply. Practitioners advising a spouse or civil partner in this situation should ensure that the spouse or civil partner elects within the relevant period of one year and should not wait for the personal representatives to serve a Notice of the Right on the spouse or civil partner. If the spouse or civil partner wishes to have the dwelling appropriated, then it is best to make a pre-emptive move and serve the notice of requirement on the personal representatives even before they serve a Notice on the spouse or civil partner.

It shall be the duty of the personal representatives to notify the spouse or civil partner in writing of the right of election conferred by this section.

The right shall not be exercisable after the expiration of six months from the receipt by the spouse of such notification or one year from the first taking out of representation of the deceased's estate, whichever is the later.

NOTE: Succession Act 1965, s 56 4) & (5a) as amended by the Civil Partnership and Certain Rights and Obligations of Cohabitants Act 2010, s (67)(a)

"Application to prohibit appropriation of any part of the estate by Personal Representative:-

Six weeks from the receipt of the notice of appropriation

[Succession Act 1965, s 55(3)]

Section 67A(3) Applications (Claim by Issue of Civil Partner)

Six Months from the Date of the Grant of Representation

This application is introduced in s 67A inserted into the Succession Act by s 70 of the Civil Partnership and Certain Rights and Obligations of Cohabitants Act 2010 in cases of a deceased who dies intestate leaving a civil partner and issue.

The issue of the intestate may apply to the court for provision to be made for the issue out of the intestate's estate only if the court is of the opinion that it would be unjust not to make the order after considering factors as set out in s 67A (3) to (7) of the Civil Partnership and Certain Rights and Obligations of Cohabitants Act 2010.

(7) An order under this section shall not be made except on an application made within 6 months from the first taking out of representation of the deceased's estate.

NOTE: Succession Act 1965, s 67A(7) inserted by the Civil Partnership and Certain Rights and Obligations of Cohabitants Act 2010, s (73).

Section 117 Applications (Claim by Child to Estate of Parent)

Six Months from Date of Grant of Representation

The time limit for these applications was reduced from one year to six months and it is vital that proceedings are issued immediately in order to protect the interests of the clients.

If for some reason the clients are unaware of the identity of the deceased's solicitors who will be acting in the administration of the Estate, it is advisable then to lodge a caveat in the Probate Office which of course will be warned by the solicitors acting for the Estate. Practitioners should have the proceedings drafted immediately and ready to be issued and served as soon as the Grant of Probate issues.

(6) An order under this section shall not be made except on an application made within [six] months from the first taking out of representation of the deceased's estate.

NOTE: Succession Act 1965, s 117 (6) amended by Family Law (Divorce) Act 1996, s 46.

Time Allowed for Distribution of Estate

Executors One Year from Date of Death

The personal representatives have a duty to administer the estate in an efficient and timely manner and must not delay. An action to compel administration cannot be brought against the Personal Representative for a period of one year from the date of death. This is also known as "the executors year". However, such limit does not apply to a creditor of the estate.

62.—(1) The personal representatives of a deceased person shall distribute his estate as soon after his death as is reasonably practicable having regard to the nature of the estate, the manner in which it is required to be distributed and all other relevant circumstances, but proceedings against the personal representatives in respect of their failure to distribute shall not, without leave of the court, be brought before the expiration of one year from the date of the death of the deceased.

(2) Nothing in this section shall prejudice or affect the rights of creditors of a deceased person to bring proceedings against his personal representatives before the expiration of one year from his death.

NOTE: Succession Act 1965, s 62.

Chapter 8

Disclaimers

Introduction

A beneficiary cannot be forced to accept a gift under a Will or on an intestacy and he may disclaim the gift by deed of disclaimer or may be deemed to have disclaimed by his conduct. Most gifts are disclaimed from an altruistic motive where the disclaiming by one beneficiary will benefit a more needy beneficiary.

When to Disclaim

A beneficiary must disclaim before he has received any benefit from the gift and cannot withdraw the disclaimer when another beneficiary has received benefit from the gift as a result of the disclaimer. See *Re Cranstoun* [1949] Ch. 523.

Effect of Disclaimer

Where there is a disclaimer the general rules of law (Succession Act 1965 as amended) establish who is to benefit.

Once the beneficiary disclaims the gift, the gift falls into the residue of the Will and is distributed to the residuary legatees.

In the absence of a residuary clause or in the event of a gift of part of the residue being disclaimed the gift will be distributed on intestacy.

The disclaimed gift is treated as a failed gift which has lapsed.

A gift or inheritance can be disclaimed for consideration if that consideration moves from the residue of the estate and consequently the residue is then reduced by the amount of the consideration.

Section 12 of the Capital Acquisitions Tax Consolidation Act 2003 deals with the effect and consequences of disclaimers of benefits.

The section only applies where a person disclaims a benefit.

A bequest cannot be disclaimed in favour of another named beneficiary. This is not a disclaimer but is effectively a gift to a third party, by the beneficiary of the bequest received and is treated by the Revenue for CAT purposes as a benefit passing from the deceased to the beneficiary and a further gift passing from the disclaiming beneficiary to the named third party thus giving rise to two charges of CAT.

12.—(1) If –

    (*a*) (i) a benefit under a will or an intestacy, or

        (ii) an entitlement to an interest in settled property,

    is disclaimed;

(*b*) a claim –

> (i) under a purported will in respect of which a grant of representation (within the meaning of the Succession Act 1965) was not issued, or

> (ii) under an alleged intestacy where a will exists in respect of which such a grant was issued,

> is waived; or

(*c*) a right under Part IX of the Succession Act 1965 , or any analogous right under the law of another territory, is renounced, disclaimed, elected against or lapses,

any liability to tax in respect of such benefit, entitlement, claim or right shall cease as if such benefit, entitlement, claim or right, as the case may be, had not existed.

(2) Notwithstanding anything contained in this Act –

(*a*) a disclaimer of a benefit under a will or intestacy or of an entitlement to an interest in settled property;

(*b*) the waiver of a claim –

> (i) under a purported will in respect of which a grant of representation (within the meaning of the Succession Act 1965) was not issued, or

> (ii) under an alleged intestacy where a will exists in respect of which such a grant issued; or

(*c*) (i) the renunciation or disclaimer of,

    (ii) the election against, or

    (iii) the lapse of,

    a right under Part IX of the Succession Act 1965, or any analogous right under the law of another territory,

is not a disposition for the purposes of this Act.

(3) *Subsection (1)* shall not apply to the extent of the amount of any consideration in money or money's worth received for the disclaimer, renunciation, election or lapse or for the waiver of a claim; and the receipt of such consideration is deemed to be a gift or an inheritance, as the case may be, in respect of which no consideration was paid by the donee or successor and which was derived from the disponer who provided the property in relation to which the benefit, entitlement, claim or right referred to in *subsection (1)*, arose.

NOTE: Capital Acquisitions Tax Consolidation Act 2003, s 12.

Effect of Disclaimer in Various Situations

1. Where a person disclaims a benefit they no longer have a liability to CAT in respect of that disclaimed benefit.

2. A disclaimer is not itself a disposition for CAT purposes.

3. A person can disclaim for consideration. The consideration is then treated as a benefit moving from the original disponer to the person disclaiming (i.e. a substituted gift or inheritance). See example 4

4. A disclaimer in favour of a named person is considered as an acquisition and a subsequent disposal and therefore there is a double charge to CAT.

5. A disclaimed legacy falls into residue.

6. If a residuary legatee disclaims, the residue is distributed as if there was an intestacy as regards that legatee's share of the residue.

7. A share of the residue may be disclaimed. That share is then distributed as on intestacy. A person who therefore inherits a half-share of the residue can disclaim that half-share.

8. A person cannot partially disclaim the residue or partially disclaim a share of the residue.

9. A person may however disclaim one of several legacies, either pecuniary or specific.

10. If a life interest or other limited interest is disclaimed the remainder interest falls in immediately.

Examples

Example 1: Disclaiming a specific bequest

Peter, a widower with one child, a daughter Gillian, dies testate. He leaves a pecuniary legacy of €80,000 to his brother Gordon and the residue of his estate to Gillian.

Gordon recently won the lotto and decides to disclaim the legacy to him of €80,000.

The legacy falls into the residue of the estate and is inherited by Gillian, together with the residue of the estate.

Gordon has no liability to CAT as he has disclaimed the benefit to him.

Gillian has inherited the entire estate from her father Peter and has taken no benefit from Gordon.

Example 2: Disclaiming a share of the residue

Jane, a widow dies testate and leaves the residue of her estate equally to her 3 children Phil, Brian and Bob.

Bob, who is in far better circumstances that the other two disclaims his one-third share of the residue under the will, which one-third share then passes by intestacy equally to the three children as to a one-ninth share each. Bob must also disclaim his one-ninth share of the residue passing under the partial intestacy and then this one-ninth share then passes equally to Phil and Brian.

Phil and Brian each end up inheriting a half-share of the estate from Jane, and Bob is regarded as inheriting nothing.

Example 3: Attempted disclaimer in favour of a named person

John inherits a house under the will of his cousin, Jim but disclaims the inheritance of the house in favour of his brother Denis.

Since it is not possible to disclaim a benefit in favour of somebody else, this is an inheritance taken by John from Jim and then a separate gift of the house by John to Denis. Therefore inheritance tax will arise on the bequest from Jim and gift tax on the gift to Denis.

Example 4: **Disclaiming for consideration from the estate**

Primrose dies and leaves her farm valued at €750,000 to her son Steven and the residue of her estate to her daughter June.

Steven has no interest in farming, decides to disclaim the bequest of the farm to him in consideration of a payment to him of €350,000 from the estate.

Steven is then regarded as taking an inheritance of €350,000 from his mother Primrose.

June is then treated as taking an inheritance from her mother Primrose of the farm together with the residue of the estate, less the €350,000 passing to Steven.

Chapter 9

Discretionary Trusts

Introduction

A discretionary trust is one which does not give a beneficiary any right to part of the capital or the income of the trust property, but vests in the trustees a discretionary power to pay same to the beneficiary, or apply to the beneficiary's benefit, such part of the income or capital as they think fit. Therefore, no beneficiary has the right to any part of the trust property and receives, if anything at all, only that portion of the property which the trustees see fit to give him.

Over the years discretionary trusts have been widely used as mechanisms to keep the property from spendthrift children, to provide for incapacitated persons and as tax avoidance vehicles. The beneficiaries of the trust could not get their hands on the property and dissipate the assets. These trusts had the effect of postponing any liability to CAT until a distribution was made. This type of trust and its use in estates was recognised by the Revenue Commissioners with the enactment of the Capital Acquisitions Tax Act 1976 (now repealed) and a discretionary trust in the 1976 Act was defined as:

"Discretionary Trust" means any trust whereby, or by virtue or in consequence of which, property is held on trust to

> apply, or with a power to apply, the income or capital or part of the income or capital of the property for the benefit of any person or persons of any one or more of a number or of a class of persons whether at the discretion of trustees or any other person and notwithstanding that there may be a power to accumulate all or any part of the income.

Subsequent to the commencement of the Capital Acquisitions Tax Act the discretionary trust became widely used. This was as a result of the high level of taxation and possibly due to the fact that dispositions between spouses were then subject to CAT. The Revenue were unhappy at the way in which discretionary trusts were being used and the Finance Act of 1984 introduced a discretionary trust tax and changed the definition of discretionary trust as follows:

> "discretionary trust" means any trust whereby, or by virtue or in consequence of which, property is held on trust [to accumulate the income or part of the income of the property, or any trust whereby, or by virtue or in consequence of which, property (other than property to which for the time being a person is beneficially entitled for an interest in possession) is held on trust],to apply, or with a power to apply, the income or capital or part of the income or capital of the property for the benefit of any person or persons or of any one or more of a number or of a class of persons whether at the discretion of trustees or any other person and notwithstanding that there may be a power to accumulate all or any part of the income
>
> NOTE: Capital Acquisitions Tax Act 1976, s 2, as amended by Finance Act 1984, s 105.

This definition with minor amendments was then used in the Capital Acquisitions Tax Consolidation Act 2003 and is set out in s 2 of that Act:

> "discretionary trust" means any trust whereby, or by virtue or in consequence of which –
>
> (*a*) property is held on trust to accumulate the income or part of the income of the property, or
>
> (*b*) property (other than property to which for the time being a person is beneficially entitled for an interest in possession) is held on trust to apply, or with a power to apply, the income or capital or part of the income or capital of the property for the benefit of any person or persons or of any one or more of a number or of a class of persons whether at the discretion of trustees or any other person and notwithstanding that there may be a power to accumulate all or any part of the income;

It should be noted that the definition was widened and moved from the strict legal definition of a discretionary trust and expanded it to include a trust whereby property is held on trust to accumulate the income whether or not the trustees have any discretionary power as in the normal discretionary trust.

Practitioners, therefore, when drafting Wills which include the creation of a trust should be very careful in the wording to ensure that they do not inadvertently create a discretionary trust within the meaning of the definition in the 2003 Act. Note that sub sections (a) and (b) are disjunctive and consequently alternatives.

Creation of Discretionary Trust

Trusts can be created *inter vivos* during a person's lifetime or they can be created by Will, taking effect after a person's death. Tax implications can arise on the set up of the trust, during the life of the trust, when appointments are made from the trust and on final distribution of all the trust assets.

In addition to the usual taxes that may apply during the course of a trust, in the case of a "discretionary trust", discretionary trust tax may also apply.

Discretionary Trust Tax

Discretionary trust tax consists of an initial levy and an annual levy. There is an exemption for trusts created exclusively for charitable purposes, certain superannuation schemes, incapacitated persons or the upkeep of certain houses. There is no relief for business assets, agricultural assets or government stocks or securities held in such a trust. Discretionary trust tax when it arises applies to the entire value of the fund.

Discretionary Trusts Exempt from Discretionary Trust Tax

Certain discretionary trusts are exempt from the provisions of discretionary trust tax where it is shown to the satisfaction of the Revenue Commissioners that the trust was created exclusively for one of the following purposes:

1. For public or charitable purposes in the State or Northern Ireland;

2. For certain approved superannuation schemes;

3. For the benefit of individuals incapable of maintaining their own affairs;

4. For the upkeep of certain homes, houses or gardens referred to in the Finance Act 1978, s 39.

Capital Acquisitions Tax Consolidation Act 2003, s 17.

Initial Levy

The initial levy is a once off charge and applies to the trust fund at a rate of 6%.

This is now set out in Chapter 2 of the Capital Acquisitions Tax Consolidation Act 2003.

The initial levy applies to discretionary trusts on the latest of the following dates and must be paid within three months of that date.

- The date on which the property becomes subject to the discretionary trust; or

- The date of death of the settlor; or

- The date of the youngest principal object's 21st birthday.

A "principal object" is defined as:

- The spouse of the disponer,

- The children of the disponer; and

- The minor children of a pre-deceased child of the disponer.

A grandchild (unless a minor child of a deceased child) or a niece or nephew are not principal objects.

Refund

Where within five years of the death of the disponer or within five years of the youngest of the principal objects reaching 21 years the trust is wound up, a rate of 3% is used to compute the tax and a refund may be claimed from the Revenue. The refund must be claimed because in practice the Revenue Commissioners will not automatically make the refund (Capital Acquisitions Tax Consolidation Act 2003, s 18(3)).

Annual Levy

This levy was introduced in 1986 and it applies to the trust fund at a rate of 1%. The annual levy commences the year after the year in which the initial levy is charged. The annual levy is charged on 31 December every year (previously 6 April, but changed in Finance Act 2006) and must be paid within three months of that date (Capital Acquisitions Tax Consolidation Act 2003, ss 19–25).

Testators contemplating setting up a trust for their children should be advised of discretionary trust tax. Many parents with substantial estates generally wish to prevent the assets from vesting in their children until the youngest is at least 25. Consequently, if they wish to create a discretionary trust they must be advised that discretionary trust tax is charged when the youngest principal object, usually a child, is 21 if they are insisting on a later vesting age.

It should be noted that a trust set up exclusively for persons under 18, even if they are not principal objects, will be exempt from discretionary trust tax. A minor is regarded as being a person with incapacity for the purposes of the exemption in Capital Acquisitions Tax Consolidation Act 2003, s 17(1)(d).

Discretionary Trusts For Incapacitated Persons

The Capital Acquisitions Tax Consolidation Act 2003, s 17 grants an exemption from discretionary trust tax where the discretionary trust is set up exclusively for one or more incapacitated persons. The section defines an incapacitated person as one who is "because of age or improvidence, or of physical, mental or legal incapacity, incapable of managing that individual or those individuals' affairs". This includes a minor, even if that minor is not a principal object.

The exemption will only apply where the discretionary trust has been exclusively set up for the incapacitated person and no other persons.

When creating a trust in a Will it is very important to ascertain if a discretionary trust is really necessary and care should be taken not to create one unintentionally. Remember, a discretionary trust is one of the following:

(a) A trust which empowers the trustees to accumulate the income of the trust or;

(b) A trust which vests a discretion in the trustees as to when and how the trust property may be distributed;

When drafting such a trust for the children of the settlor ensure that the trust ends when the youngest child reaches its 21st birthday if the settlor wishes to avoid discretionary trust tax.

Chapter 10

Capital Acquisitions Tax (CAT)

A very important element of advising and dealing with probate and administration of estates for a client is capital acquisitions tax on gifts and inheritances. Returns, detailing the property and a calculation of the tax, must be made to the Revenue in the following cases:

(a) if the gift or inheritance, together with the aggregation of previous taxable values of previous taxable gifts taken on or after the 5th December 1991, amounts to 80% or greater of the persons threshold amount or;

(b) if the Revenue have served a notice on the person requiring the delivery of a return.

> the aggregate of the taxable values of all taxable gifts taken by the donee on or after 5 December 1991, which have the same group threshold (as defined in *Schedule 2*) as that other gift, exceeds an amount which is 80 per cent of the threshold amount (as defined in *Schedule 2*) which applies in the computation of tax on that aggregate, or

> the donee or, in a case to which section 32 (2) applies, the transferee (within the meaning of, and to the extent provided for by, that section) is required by notice in writing by the Commissioners to deliver a return [Capital Acquisitions Tax Consolidation Act 2003, s 46 (4)(A) and (B)].

Property Liable to CAT

The following property is liable to CAT:

1. All property in the State is liable to gift/inheritance tax;

2. Assets outside of the State are subject to gift/inheritance tax if:

   (a) the disponer is resident or ordinarily resident in the State at the date of the disposition, or

   (b) the beneficiary is resident or ordinarily resident in the State at the date of the gift or inheritance, or

   (c) in the case of appointments of gifts out of discretionary trusts, the disponer is resident or ordinarily resident in the State at

      (i) the date of the gift, or

      (ii) the date of the disposition, i.e. the date the trust was created, or

      (iii) in the case of a gift taken after the date of death of the disponer, at the date of his/her death.

When is the Tax Payable

A CAT return to the Revenue must be made and any tax due paid within a specified period of a date called the valuation date.

Valuation Date

The Valuation Date is the date on which the market value of the property comprising the gift/inheritance is established.

1. In the case of a Gift, the Valuation Date is normally the date of the gift.

2. In the case of an Inheritance, the Valuation Date is normally the earliest of the following dates:

    (a) the date the subject matter of the inheritance can be retained for the benefit of the beneficiary;

    (b) the date it is actually retained for the benefit of the beneficiary;

    (c) the date it is transferred or paid over to the beneficiary.

3. The Valuation Date will normally be the date of death in the following circumstances:

    (a) gift made in contemplation of death (*Donatio Mortis Causa*);

    (b) where a power of revocation has not been exercised;

    (c) where property passes by survivorship or under a trust.

Property held by joint tenancy which passes by the right of survivorship, (*jus accrescendi*) to the surviving joint tenants does not form part of a deceased's estate for the purpose of the Succession Act 1965 but does form part of the estate for the purposes of Capital Acquisitions Tax and must be included in any necessary return to the Revenue.

The following examples illustrate the Valuation Date for various benefits.

Example 1: Valuation Date of an inheritance taken under a Will

David, a divorcee, made the following bequests in his will:

(a) house to his partner, Jane, who was residing with him;

(b) €25,000 pecuniary legacy, to his brother Jack;

(c) the residue of his estate, consisting of quoted shares and bank accounts, to his partner Jane

The Valuation Date for each inheritance would normally be:

1. House, date of death, Jane is living in and has possession of the house;

2. Pecuniary legacy, the date of grant of probate, unless the Bank paid the legacy to Jack prior to that date, the date of payment would be the valuation date;

3. the date of grant of probate in respect of the residue, since the shares could not be sold and the accounts closed until the issue of the grant.

Example 2: **Intestacy**

In the case of an intestacy, the Valuation Date of each inheritance taken by the next-of-kin would normally be the date of grant of administration.

Example 3: **Valuation Date of Gift and Inheritance taken under a Deed**

Jack a widower with no issue, on his retirement from business, executed a deed transferring his house and farm as follows:

(a) to his sister Jane, for her life (gift);

(b) on her death to his nephew Michael absolutely (this will be an inheritance taken by Michael from his uncle Jack on Jane's death).

The respective Valuation Dates are as follows:

1. the date of the deed in respect of the gift of a life interest to Jane;

2. the date of Janes's death in the case of the inheritance taken by Michael.

Importance of Valuation Date

The market value of the property, the subject of the benefit, is ascertained as at the valuation date. This is now highly significant where there have been huge falls in the values of property and particularly shares.

Example

Mary, a spinster without children dies in December 2007 leaving:

(a) a house, to be sold and proceeds divided in certain shares, value at date of death €500,000.00;

(b) shares in Irish Banks, value at date of death €200,000.00

(c) Shares in various UK companies, value at date of death €150,000.00

Total value of the estate at the date of death €850,000.00.

The original of her will is lost and application has to be made to Court to have a copy will admitted to probate. This delays probate and the grant does not issue until February 2009 when the values are as follows:

(a) House €300,000.00

(b) Irish bank shares €5,000.00

(c) UK shares €15,000.00

The valuation date for all of these assets is the date of the grant of probate since house or shares could not be sold until without same. The total value of the estate at the valuation date is €330,000.00. This is a significant reduction. Of course the converse can also happen.

1. Sole asset 20 acres of farmland at Blackacre, value at date of death €150,000.00.

2. Land rezoned six months after death, low density housing value increases to €2,000,000.00.

3. Grant issues six months after rezoning.

4. Total value of estate for CAT purposes €2,000,000.00 as opposed to €150,000.00.

In all cases the valuation date may be agreed in writing between the Commissioners and the accountable person or his agent.

Subject to subsection (7), the valuation date of a taxable gift is the date of the gift.

(2) The valuation date of a taxable inheritance is the date of death of the deceased person on whose death the inheritance is taken if the successor or any person in right of the successor or on that successor's behalf takes the inheritance –

(*a*) as a *donatio mortis causa*, or

(*b*) by reason of the failure to exercise a power of revocation.

(3) If a gift becomes an inheritance by reason of its being taken under a disposition where the date of the disposition

is within 2 years prior to the death of the disponer, the valuation date of the inheritance is determined as if it were a gift.

(4) The valuation date of a taxable inheritance, other than a taxable inheritance referred to in subsection (2) or (3), is the earliest date of the following:

(*a*) the earliest date on which a personal representative or trustee or the successor or any other person is entitled to retain the subject matter of the inheritance for the benefit of the successor or of any person in right of the successor or on that successor's behalf, (*b*) the date on which the subject matter of the inheritance is so retained, or

(*c*) the date of delivery, payment or other satisfaction or discharge of the subject matter of the inheritance to the successor or for that successor's benefit or to or for the benefit of any person in right of the successor or on that successor's behalf.

(5) If any part of a taxable inheritance referred to in subsection (4) may be retained, or is retained, delivered, paid or otherwise satisfied, whether by means of part payment, advancement, payment on account or in any manner whatever, before any other part or parts of such inheritance, the appropriate valuation date for each part of the inheritance is determined in accordance with that subsection as if each such part respectively were a separate inheritance.

(6) The Commissioners may give to an accountable person a notice in writing of the date determined by them to be the valuation date in respect of the whole or any part of an

inheritance, and, subject to any decision on appeal pursuant to subsection (9), the date so determined is deemed to be the valuation date.

(7) If a taxable inheritance referred to in subsection (4) or *(5)* is disposed of, ceases or comes to an end before the valuation date referred to in those subsections in such circumstances as to give rise to a taxable gift, the valuation date in respect of such taxable gift is the same date as the valuation date of the taxable inheritance.

(8) Notwithstanding anything contained in this section, the Commissioners may, in case of doubt, with the agreement in writing of the accountable person or that person's agent, determine the valuation date of the whole or any part of any taxable inheritance and the valuation date so determined is substituted for the valuation date which would otherwise be applicable by virtue of this section.

(9) An appeal shall lie against any determination made by the Commissioners under subsection (6) and section 67 shall apply, with any necessary modifications, in relation to an appeal under this subsection as it applies in relation to an appeal against an assessment of tax.

[Capital Acquisitions Tax Consolidation Act 2003, s 30].

File and Pay

The Finance Act 2010 introduces a fixed pay and file date for CAT of 31 October, to align with the Income Tax pay and file deadline, with some added time being given (as for Income Tax) to payments/returns made via Revenue's On-line Service (ROS). All gifts and inheritances with a valuation date in the 12 month period ending on the previous 31 August will be included in the return to be filed by 31 October. That means where the valuation date arises between 1 January and 31 August, the pay and file deadline would be 31 October in that year; and where the valuation date arises between 1 September and 31 December, the pay and file deadline would be 31 October in the following year.

Before the enactment of the Finance Act 2010 the period between the valuation date and the filing/payment date was generally four months. However, with the nomination of the 31 August as the year end date, the period between the valuation date and the filing/payment date will increase in most cases. At its outset, the filing period will increase from four months to 14 months. For example, where the valuation date is 1 September 2010, tax will not be due until 31 October 2011. However, the period between the valuation date and the filing/payment date in a number of cases will be less than four months (i.e. where the valuation date arises between 2 July and 31 August).

For the purposes of subsection (2) (other than in the case of an inheritance to which section 15 or 20 applies), where the relevant date occurs –

(*a*) in the period from 1 January to 31 August in any year, tax shall be paid and a return shall be delivered on or before 31 October in that year, and

(*b*) in the period from 1 September to 31 December in any year, tax shall be paid and a return shall be delivered on or before 31 October in the following year.

NOTE: Capital Acquisitions Consolidation Act 2003, s 2A inserted by the Finance Act 2010, s 147(1)(f).

Example
Valuation date 30 August 2010 File IT 38 and pay by the 31 October 2010, a period of two months but where the valuation date is a week later on the 6 September 2010 the file and pay date is the 31 October 2011 almost 14 months later.

The Finance Act 2011 changed the file and pay deadline to the 30 September. However the nominated year end date of the 31 August remains unchanged so in the above example the period of two months is reduced to one month and the period of 14 months reduced to 13.

Surcharge for Late Return of Cat

There is a surcharge payable where the return is late. A rate of 5% of the amount of tax applies up to a maximum of €12,695 where the return is two months late and a rate of 10% of the amount of tax up to a maximum of €63,485 after two months.

"Where a person fails to deliver a return on or before the specified return date, any amount of tax which would have been payable if such a return had been delivered shall be increased by an amount (in this section referred to as 'the surcharge') equal to—

(a) 5 per cent of the amount of tax, subject to a maximum increased amount of €12,695, where the return is delivered before the expiry of 2 months from the specified return date, and

(b) 10 per cent of the amount of tax subject to a maximum increased amount of €63,485, where the return is not delivered before the expiry of 2 months from the specified return date.

NOTE: Capital Acquisitions Tax Consolidation Act 2003, s 53a(3) inserted by the Finance Act 2010, s 147(1)(p)

Groups and Their Respective Applicable Thresholds

The Group thresholds are set out in the CATA 2003 schedule 2 Part 1.

The relationship between the disponer and the beneficiary at the date of the Gift or Inheritance determines the maximum tax free threshold known as the "group threshold".

The group thresholds applicable are:

Group A
Group A threshold applies where the beneficiary is

- a child, or a minor child of a deceased child of the disponer.

- The term "child" includes a stepchild or an adopted child (under the Adoption Acts).

- Minor means under the age of 18.

Parents taking an absolute inheritance from a child have a group A threshold. However, if the child took a non-exempt gift or inheritance from either parent in the previous five years, any inheritance taken by a parent from that child is exempt.

A foster child will also qualify for the Group A threshold in respect of a benefit taken on or after 6 December 2000 if s/he had been cared for and maintained, at the disponer's own expense, from a young age up to the age of 18 for period(s) amounting to at least five years and has also resided with the disponer. The five year requirement will not apply in the case of a formal fostering under the relevant Child Care Regulations where the foster child inherits on the death of a foster parent.

Claims for the relief by a foster child will have to be supported by the testimony of two witnesses (CATA 2003, schedule 2, s 9).

Group B
Group B threshold applies where the beneficiary is –

  (a) a lineal ancestor e.g. * parent or grandparent (* parent takes a Group B threshold where they take a gift or a limited interest in an inheritance);

  (b) a lineal descendant e.g. a grandchild or great-grandchild;

  (c) a brother or sister;

  (d) a child of a brother or sister of the disponer.

Group C
The group C threshold applies to "strangers" i.e. where the relationship between disponer and beneficiary falls outside either group A or group B.

NOTE

  1. Gifts or Inheritances taken from a spouse are entirely exempt regardless of the amount involved.

  2. In certain circumstances, the beneficiary may take the threshold of his/her deceased spouse where that spouse has pre-deceased the disponer and was of a nearer relationship to the disponer, e.g. a daughter-in-law of

the disponer can qualify for the group A (rather than the group C) threshold if her husband predeceased the disponer.

In certain circumstances, a grandchild can qualify for group A threshold (rather than group B) if the benefit is taken on the death of the beneficiary's surviving parent under a disposition made pre 1 April 1975 where the consideration for the disposition was the marriage of the parents of the beneficiary. The disponer is a grandparent of the beneficiary.

Adopted Child

An adopted child taking Gifts or Inheritances from a natural parent is entitled to a Group A threshold. S/he is also entitled to a Group A threshold from his/her adoptive parents (CATA 2003, schedule 2, s 10).

However, it should be noted that an adopted child does not have any rights to the natural parents' estates under the provisions of the Succession Act 1965 pertaining to children by virtue of the Status of Children Act 1987, s 3(2)(a) and (b) since from the date of adoption the child is deemed to be the child of the adopters and not of any other person.

(*a*) An adopted person shall, for the purposes of *subsection (1)* of this section, be deemed from the date of the adoption to be the child of the adopter or adopters and not the child of any other person or persons.

(*b*) In this subsection "adopted person" means a person who has been adopted under the Adoption Acts, 1952 to 1976, or, where the person has been adopted outside the

State, whose adoption is recognised by virtue of the law for the time being in force in the State.

The current rates of the various thresholds are as follows:

The indexed group thresholds for 2009, 2010 and 2011					
Group	Relationship to Disponer	Group Threshold from 1 January 2009 to 7 April 2009	Group Threshold from 8 April 2009	Group Threshold 2010 to 7 December 2010	Group Threshold 2011 from 8 December 2010
A	Son/Daughter	€542,544	€434,000	€414,799	€332,084
B	Parent*/Brother/ Sister/Niece/ Nephew/Grandchild	€54,254	€43,400	€41,481	€33,208
C	Relationship other than Group A or	€27,127	€21,700	€20,740	€16,604

*In certain circumstances a parent taking an inheritance from a child can qualify for Group A threshold.

Abolition of the status of CAT as a charge on property that has been the subject of a gift or inheritance in the previous 12 years. The Capital Acquisitions Consolidation Act 2003, s 60 made any tax due and payable in respect of a taxable gift or a taxable inheritance be and remain a charge on the property and remain charged for a period of 12 years from the date of the gift or inheritance.

Section 147(3) of the 2010 Finance Act has abolished CAT as a charge on property received as a gift or an inheritance. The section states that s 60 of the 2003 Act shall not now apply to gifts and inheritances taken before the date of the passing of the Finance Act. This now eliminates the need to apply for certificates of discharge from CAT when acting for a vendor of a property where there has been a death on the title during the previous 12 years. The abolition of the charge on property came into effect with the passing of the Finance Act 2010 and extends to all applications for certificates of discharge, including those relating to gifts and inheritances taken prior to the passing of the Act, except in cases where Revenue has already instituted proceedings for the recovery of tax on foot of the charge.

> The provisions of sections 45, 60 and 63(4) of the Principal Act as they applied any time before the passing of this Act, or any corresponding provision in a previous enactment, shall not apply to gifts and inheritances taken before the date of the passing of this Act except where the Revenue Commissioners have instituted proceedings to recover gift tax or inheritance tax before that date.
>
> [Finance Act 2010, s 147(3)].

Abolition of Secondary Accounting

The CATA 2003 extended secondary accountability to a number of other parties (e.g. personal representatives (including agents) or the donor in the case of a gift) where the beneficiary fails to pay the tax due and the person secondarily liable has control over the property passing. This secondary liability gave rise to a number of requests for certificates of personal discharge by those otherwise potentially liable in the event of default by the beneficiary.

Secondary accountability has now been abolished for inheritances and gifts by the Finance Act, 2010 and this has eliminated the need for applications for certificates of personal discharge. This change has been brought about with the enactment of the Finance Act, 2010 which changes the definition of the "accountable person".

The accountable person is now as follows:

> The person accountable for the payment of tax is –
>
> > (*a*) the donee or successor, and
> >
> > (*b*) in the case referred to in section 32(2), the transferee referred to in that subsection, to the extent referred to in that subsection.
>
> (2) The tax shall be recoverable from the person referred to in subsection (1) and the personal representative of such person, where that person has died, on whom the Commissioners have served notice in writing of the assessment of tax in accordance with section 49(4).
>
> NOTE: CATA 2003, s 45 substituted by the Finance Act 2010, s 147(1)(b).

The transferee referred to in s 32(2) is as follows:

> Where a benefit, to which a person (in this section referred to as the remainderman) is entitled under a disposition, devolves, or is disposed of, either in whole or in part, before it has become an interest in possession so that, at the time when the benefit comes into possession, it is taken, either

in whole or in part, by a person (in this section referred to as the transferee) other than the remainderman to whom it was limited by the disposition, then tax is payable, in respect of a gift or inheritance, as the case may be, of the remainderman in all respects as if, at that time, the remainderman had become beneficially entitled in possession to the full extent of the benefit limited to that remainderman under the disposition, and the transferee is the person primarily accountable for the payment of tax to the extent that the benefit is taken by that transferee.

[CATA 2003, s 32(2)].

Requirement to appoint an Irish-resident "agent" who will be responsible for pay and file procedures where beneficiaries are non-resident

Since the enactment of the Finance Act 2010 an Irish resident personal representative taking out probate or letters of administration will be appointed as an "Agent" of a non-resident beneficiary entitled to a benefit exceeding €20,000. The agent will be responsible for the pay and file requirements of the non-resident beneficiary. In this regard, the agent will be entitled to retain funds adequate to meet the CAT liability from any amounts due to the beneficiary under the control of the agent. The liability of the agent will be restricted to the extent of the funds under his/her control which are available for distribution to the beneficiary.

Where there is no Irish resident personal representative, the personal representatives must appoint a Solicitor holding a practising certificate in the State as agent prior to seeking probate or letters of administration. The Probate office is prohibited from issuing a grant unless such solicitor has been appointed.

In these circumstances the personal representative and the solicitor may have a secondary liability and in such cases these persons should apply for personal certificates of discharge when the estate is administered.

Reliefs from Capital Acquisitions Tax

There are a number of reliefs from CAT available. The practitioner should be in a position to advise on the most common of these as follows:

1. Agriculture Relief

This relief is available if the following apply:

(a) the property the subject matter of the disposition consists of agricultural property; and

(b) the donee is a farmer as defined below;

"Agricultural property" means –

(*a*) agricultural land, pasture and woodland situate in the State and crops, trees and underwood growing on such land and also includes such farm buildings, farm houses and mansion houses (together with the lands occupied with such farm buildings, farm houses and mansion houses) as are of a character appropriate to the property, and farm machinery, livestock and bloodstock on such property, and (*b*) a payment entitlement (within the meaning of Council Regulation (EC) No. 1782/2003 of 29 September 2003[23]);",

NOTE: CATA 2003, s 89(1) Amended by the Finance Act 2006, s118(1)(a)(i).

"Farmer" means –

"farmer" in relation to a donee or successor, means an individual […] in respect of whom not less than 80 per cent of the market value of the property to which the individual is beneficially entitled in possession is represented by the market value of property in the State which consists of agricultural property, and, for the purposes of this definition –

(*a*) no deduction is made from the market value of property for any debts or encumbrances (except debts or encumbrances in respect of a dwelling house which is the only or main residence of the donee or successor and which is not agricultural property), and

NOTE: CATA 2003, s 89(1) amended by the Finance Act 2006, s 118(1)(a)(i) and s 89 (1)(a) Substituted by the Finance Act 2007, s 117(1).

This effectively means that the beneficiary is a farmer is after taking the disposition the beneficiary's agricultural assets (at the valuation date) are equal to or greater in value than 80% of his/her total assets. If these conditions are satisfied then the market value of the agricultural property is reduced by 90% and this is the amount that the beneficiary is deemed to have received for CAT purposes. CAT is then calculated in the normal manner. However there are clawbacks if the property is sold within six years and not replaced with other agricultural property.

2. Small Gift Exemption

An individual is permitted to receive up to €3,000 per tax year free of CAT from any person. This is known as the small gift exemption and applies to gifts only and not inheritances. However, if the gift becomes an inheritance by virtue of the death of the disponer within two years of the gift, the exemption will continue to apply (CATA 2003, s 69 Amended by the Finance Act 2003, s 149).

3. Business Property Relief

This relief applies to gifts or inheritances of "relevant business property" as defined below.

There are strict conditions to be satisfied in order for the relief to apply including, inter alia, ownership and control tests for the beneficiary to satisfy following the gift or inheritance. Where the relief applies the taxable value of the relevant business property is reduced by 90%. There is a clawback of the relief if the property is disposed of within six years.

However, where some or all of the relevant business property is sold within six years of the gift or inheritance and the sale proceeds are reinvested in further qualifying relevant business property there is no clawback of the relief.

In this Chapter and subject to the following provisions of this section and to sections 94, 96 and 100(4) "relevant business property" means, in relation to a gift or inheritance, any one or more of the following, that is:

(*a*) property consisting of a business or interest in a business.

(*b*) unquoted shares in or securities of a company whether incorporated in the State or otherwise to which paragraph (c) does not relate, and which on the valuation date (either by themselves alone or together with other shares or securities in that company in the absolute beneficial ownership of the donee or successor on that date) give control of powers of voting on all questions affecting the company as a whole which if exercised would yield more than 25 per cent of the votes capable of being exercised on those shares,

(*c*) unquoted shares in or securities of a company whether incorporated in the State or otherwise which

is, on the valuation date (after the taking of the gift or inheritance), a company controlled by the donee or successor within the meaning of section 27,

(*d*) unquoted shares in or securities of a company whether incorporated in the State or otherwise which do not fall within paragraph (b) or (c) and which on the valuation date (either by themselves alone or together with other shares or securities in that company in the absolute beneficial ownership of the donee or successor on that date) have an aggregate nominal value which represents 10 per cent or more of the aggregate nominal value of the entire share capital and securities of the company on condition that the donee or successor has been a full-time working officer or employee of the company, or if that company is a member of a group, of one or more companies which are members of the group, throughout the period of 5 years ending on the date of the gift or inheritance,

(*e*) any land or building, machinery or plant which, immediately before the gift or inheritance, was used wholly or mainly for the purposes of a business carried on by a company of which the disponer then had control or by a partnership of which the disponer then was a partner and for the purposes of this paragraph a person is deemed to have control of a company at any time if that person then had control of powers of voting on all questions affecting the company as a whole which if exercised would have yielded a majority of the votes capable of being exercised on all such questions,

(*f*) quoted shares in or securities of a company which, but for the fact that they are quoted, would be shares or securities to which paragraph (b), (c) or (d) would relate on condition that such shares or securities, or other shares in or securities of the same company which are represented by those shares or securities, were in the beneficial ownership of the disponer immediately prior to the disposition and were unquoted at the date of the commencement of that beneficial ownership or at 23 May 1994, whichever is the later date.

(2) Where a company has shares or securities of any class giving powers of voting limited to either or both –

(*a*) the question of winding-up the company, and

(*b*) any question primarily affecting shares or securities of that class, the reference in subsection (1) to all questions affecting the company as a whole has effect as a reference to all such questions except any in relation to which those powers are capable of being exercised.

(3) A business or interest in a business, or shares in or securities of a company, is not relevant business property if the business or, as the case may be, the business carried on by the company consists wholly or mainly of one or more of the following, that is, dealing in currencies, securities, stocks or shares, land or buildings, or making or holding investments.

(4) Subsection (3) shall not apply to shares in or securities of a company if –

(*a*) the business of the company consists wholly or mainly in being a holding company of one or more

companies whose business does not fall within that subsection, or

(*b*) the value of those shares or securities, without having regard to the provisions of section 99, is wholly or mainly attributable, directly or indirectly, to businesses that do not fall within that subsection.

(5) Any land, building, machinery or plant used wholly or mainly for the purposes of a business carried on as mentioned in subsection (1)(e) is not relevant business property in relation to a gift or inheritance, unless the disponer's interest in the business is, or shares in or securities of the

company carrying on the business immediately before the gift or inheritance are, relevant business property in relation to the gift or inheritance or in relation to a simultaneous gift or inheritance taken by the same donee or successor.

(6) The references to a disponer in subsections (1)(e) and (5) include a reference to a person in whom the land, building, machinery or plant concerned is vested for a beneficial interest in possession immediately before the gift or inheritance.

(7) Where shares or securities are vested in the trustees of a settlement, any powers of voting which they give to the trustees of the settlement are, for the purposes of subsection (1)(e), deemed to be given to the person beneficially entitled in possession to the shares or securities except in a case where no individual is so entitled.

NOTE: CATA 2003, s 93 as amended by the Finance Act 2004, s 78.

Clawback Period in Respect of Development Land

Where land which had development potential at the date of the gift or inheritance and qualified for relief is disposed of by the donee in the period commencing six years after the date of the gift/inheritance and ending 10 years after that date, the relief granted will be clawed back in respect of the development value of the land at the date of the gift/inheritance. This provision applies in respect of gifts and inheritances taken on or after 2 February 2006 (and from 1 January 2005 in the case of the EU Single Farm Payment Entitlement). To qualify for the relief the relevant business property must have been owned for a continuous period of five years prior to the date of the gift/inheritance. If the gift/inheritance is taken on the death of the disponer the relevant period is two years prior to the date of the gift/inheritance.

"development land" means land in the State, the market value of which at the date of a gift or inheritance exceeds the current use value of that land at that date, and includes shares deriving their value in whole or in part from such land;

NOTE: CATA 2003, s 102 (A)(1) as inserted by the Finance Act 2006, s 118(b).

4. Dwellinghouse Relief

This relief is granted under s 86 of the 2003 Act and allows the disposal of a dwellinghouse free of CAT provided:

(a) the donee or the successor continuously occupied the dwellinghouse as his or her only or main residence for the three years immediately preceding the gift or inheritance;

(b) is not (at the date of the gift or inheritance) beneficially entitled to any other dwellinghouse or to any other interest in any other dwellinghouse (unless he or she has reached the age of 55 years at the date of the gift or inheritance);

(c) continues to occupy the dwellinghouse as that donee's (or successor's) only or main residence for six years following the gift or inheritance.

The Finance Act 2007, s 116 introduced certain restrictions on the relief only in relation to gifts as follows:

(i) in relation to the three-year period of occupancy, any period whereby the donee and the donor occupied the dwelling will be disregarded for the purpose of the relief, unless they lived together due to the dependence of the donor or the donee by reason of old age or infirmity; and

(ii) the disponer must own the dwellinghouse for the three year period, therefore ruling out gifts from certain entities e.g. companies or discretionary trusts.

The above restrictions only apply in relation to gifts of the property and not inheritances. The exemption may be withdrawn where the donee or successor disposes of the dwellinghouse within the six year period. However, the clawback will not apply where the proceeds of sale are reinvested in certain residential property and where certain conditions are met. Where replacement property is the subject of a gift on or after 1 February 2007, the period of occupancy of the replaced property by the recipient will only be taken into account where the replaced property was also owned by the disponer prior to the date of the gift (previously where a parent gifted a property to a child to replace the child's own property, the child could count the period of occupation in their own dwellinghouse for the purposes of the three out of four year occupancy rule). Where this exemption is claimed and subsequent events give rise to a clawback, interest on the tax due will run from the date of the event giving rise to the clawback and not the original date of the inheritance/gift.

"Dwelling-house" means –

> (*a*) a building or part (including an appropriate part within the meaning of section 5 *(5)*) of a building which was used or was suitable for use as a dwelling, and
>
> (*b*) the curtilage of the dwelling-house up to an area (exclusive of the site of the dwelling-house) of one acre but if the area of the curtilage (exclusive of the site of the dwelling-house) exceeds one acre then the part which comes within this definition is the part which, if the remainder were separately occupied, would be the most suitable for occupation and enjoyment with the dwelling-house;
>
> [CATA 2003, s 86(1)].

5. Capital Gains Tax (CGT) / Capital Acquisitions Tax Set-Off

Where CGT and CAT arise on the happening of the same event, s 104 of the 2003 Act, amended by the Finance Act 2006 s 119, provides that the CGT paid may be deducted from the corresponding CAT liability as a credit against the CAT liability. The relief is lost if the property the subject matter of the gift or inheritance is sold within two years of the gift or inheritance.

This relief could be availed of say, where a parent gifts an investment property to a child and the investment property is retained by the child for two years from the date of the gift. The parent is deemed to have made a disposal for CGT purposes and CGT could arise. The child could have a CAT liability in respect of the gift.

As the CGT and CAT arise on the same event, the CGT paid may be offset against the CAT.

6. Spousal Exemption

Gifts and inheritances between spouses are exempt from CAT. Sections 70 and 71 of the 2003 Act.

7. Parental Exemption

Section 79 of the 2003 Act grants an exemption from CAT to parents of a donor where the parents take an inheritance from a child on that child's death if within a period of five years immediately preceding his or her death the child had taken a non-exempt gift or inheritance from either or both parents.

> Notwithstanding any other provision of this Act, an inheritance taken by a person from a disponer is, where –
>
> > (*a*) that person is a parent of that disponer, and
> >
> > (*b*) the date of the inheritance is the date of death of that disponer,
>
> exempt from tax and is not taken into account in computing tax if that disponer took a non-exempt gift or
>
> inheritance from either or both of that disponer's parents within the period of 5 years immediately prior to the date of death of that disponer.
>
> [CATA 2003, s 79].

Aggregation of Gifts and Rules for Calculation of Capital Acquisitions Tax

Previous gifts or inheritances taken by a donee within the same group threshold are aggregated together for the purposes of calculating the amount of tax due.

The tax chargeable on the taxable value of a taxable gift or a taxable inheritance (in this Schedule referred to as the first-mentioned gift or inheritance) taken by a donee or successor shall be of an amount equal to the amount by which the tax computed on aggregate A exceeds the tax computed on aggregate B, where –

(*a*) aggregate A is the aggregate of the following:

(i) the taxable value of the first-mentioned gift or inheritance, and

(ii) the taxable value of each taxable gift and taxable inheritance taken previously by that donee or successor on or after 5 December 1991, which has the same group threshold as the first-mentioned gift or inheritance,

(*b*) aggregate B is the aggregate of the taxable values of all such taxable gifts and taxable inheritances so previously taken which have the same group threshold as the first-mentioned gift or inheritance, and

(*c*) the tax on an aggregate is computed at the rate or rates of tax applicable under the Table to that aggregate, but where –

> (i) in a case where no such taxable gift or taxable inheritance was so previously taken, the amount of the tax computed on aggregate B shall be deemed to be nil, and
>
> (ii) the amount of an aggregate that comprises only a single taxable value shall be equal to that value.
>
> [CATA 2003, Schedule 2 Part 1, s 3].

Rules

The rules as applied by the Revenue in calculating the tax are set out as follows:

NOTE
The aggregation rules applicable to a particular inheritance or gift are those which applied at the date of death or the date of gift. The Valuation Date is not relevant to aggregation rules.

Benefits taken on or after 5th December 2001:
All benefits taken from the same Group Threshold since 5 December 1991 are added together to calculate the tax on the latest benefit.

Calculation in respect of the latest of a series of benefits taken since 1991:

1. Aggregate all prior benefits within the same group threshold as the current benefit with the current benefit and calculate the tax on the total.

2. Aggregate all prior benefits within the same group threshold as the current benefits, excluding the current benefit and calculate the tax on the total.

3. Subtract tax at (2) from tax a (1) – this gives tax referable to the current benefit.

This calculation applies where aggregation applies in relation to same group/class threshold only.

Benefits taken between 1 December 1999 and 4 December 2001 inclusive:

All benefits taken from the same Group Threshold since 2 December 1988 are added together to calculate the tax on the latest benefit.

Benefits taken between 2 December 1998 and 30 November 1999 inclusive:

All benefits taken from any source (i.e. all class Thresholds) since 2 December 1988 are added together to calculate the tax on the latest benefit.

Definition of revised class threshold to be used to determine class threshold where aggregation of all benefits taken from any source applies:

"revised class threshold", in relation to a taxable gift or a taxable inheritance included in any aggregate of taxable values under the provisions of paragraph 3, means –

1. the class threshold that applies to that taxable gift or taxable inheritance, or

2. the total of the taxable values of all the taxable gifts

and taxable inheritances to which that class threshold applies and which are included in that aggregate,

whichever is the lesser:

Provided that where the revised class threshold so ascertained is less than the smallest of the class thresholds that apply in relation to all of the taxable gifts and taxable inheritances included in that aggregate, the revised class threshold shall be that smallest class threshold.

Benefits taken on or after 26 March 1984 and prior to 2 December 1998:
All Benefits taken by the beneficiary since 2 June 1982 from any source (i.e. all Class Thresholds) are added together to calculate the tax on the latest benefit.

Benefits taken after 2 June 1982 and before 26 March 1984:
All benefits taken by the beneficiary on or after 2 June, 1982 from the same group threshold are aggregated to calculate the tax on the later benefit.

Benefits taken prior to 2 June 1982:
All benefits taken after 28 February 1974 and prior to 2 June 1982 by a beneficiary are aggregated with any benefit taken since 28 February 1969 where the benefit is from the same disponer.

Chapter 11

History of Circuit Court Jurisdiction in Probate Actions

Practitioners often require to be advised as to what is the jurisdiction of the Circuit Court in probate matters. The relevant Acts have always referred to contentious matters and it appears that the jurisdiction of the Circuit Court is confined to contentious matters and it does not have jurisdiction in non-contentious matters. Therefore, applications to have a copy Will admitted to probate or to have a Will admitted to probate where a cause of death is dementia or Alzheimer's Disease or some illness which may affect the testamentary capacity of the testator are outside the jurisdiction of the Circuit Court.

There does not appear to be any provision in the enabling legislation or the Rules of the Court to enable the Circuit Court to have jurisdiction over non-contentious probate applications and these applications are more properly brought in the High Court.

The jurisdiction of the Circuit Court is mentioned in the Third Schedule of the Courts (Supplemental Provisions) Act 1961 as follows:

16.—An action in respect of the grant or revocation of the grant of probate of the will or letters of administration of the estate of a deceased person in case there is any contention in relation thereto.

Where the estate of the deceased person –

(a) in so far as it consits of personalty, exceeded at the time of his death in amount or value £2,000, exclusive of what he may have been entitled to as a trustee and not beneficially, but without deducting anything on account debts due and owing from the de ceased, or

(b) in so far as it consisted of land of which he was at the time of his death The judge of the circuit beneficially seised or possessed, exceeded the rateable valuation of £60.

17.—Proceedings for the administration of the estate of a deceased person

[Courts (Supplemental Provisions) Act, 1961 Third Schedule].

It should be noted that that Act conferred on the Circuit Court jurisdiction where the personal estate of the testator did not exceed £2,000 and insofar as the estate consisted of land, did not have a rateable valuation exceeding £60.

These provisions were repealed by the Succession Act 1965, Sch 4 Pt 2 and the jurisdiction of the Circuit Court is conferred by s 6.

6.—(1) The jurisdiction conferred on a court by this Act may be exercised by the High Court.

(2) Subject to subsection (3), the Circuit Court shall, concurrently with the High Court, have all the jurisdiction of the High Court to hear and determine proceedings of the following kinds:

(*a*) an action in respect of the grant or revocation of representation of the estate of a deceased person in case there is any contention in relation thereto;

(*b*) proceedings in respect of the administration of the estate of a deceased person or in respect of any share therein;

(*c*) any proceeding under section 56, 115, 117 or 121.

(3) Unless the necessary parties to the proceedings in a cause sign, either before or at any time during the hearing, the form of consent prescribed by rules of court, the Circuit Court shall not, by virtue of subsection (2), have jurisdiction where the estate of the deceased person –

(*a*) in so far as it consists of personal estate, exceeds at the time of his death in amount or value £5,000, exclusive of what he may have been entitled to as trustee and not beneficially, but without deducting anything on account of debts due and owing from the deceased, and

(*b*) in so far as it consists of real estate of which, at the time of his death, he was beneficially seised or possessed, exceeds the rateable valuation of £100.

> (4) The jurisdiction conferred on the Circuit Court by this section shall be exercised by the judge of the circuit where the deceased, at the time of his death, had a fixed place of abode (Succession Act 1965, s 6).

Section 6 of the Succession Act vests jurisdiction in the High Court with concurrent jurisdiction in the Circuit Court in relation to certain proceedings. The limit on the jurisdiction of the Circuit Court was, in the case of a personal estate, not exceeding £5,000 and in the case of a real estate where the rateable valuation did not exceed £100.

The Succession Act changed the definition of real estate and this definition now includes certain interests in land such as registered land and leasehold interests which prior to the enactment of the Succession Act were regarded as personalty and formed part of the personal estate of the deceased.

"**Real Estate**" is defined in the Act in s 4(1)

> "real estate" includes chattels real, and land in possession, remainder, or reversion, and every estate or interest in or over land (including real estate held by way of mortgage or security, but not including money to arise under a trust for sale of land, or money secured or charged on land);

It should be noted that by virtue of section 14 of the Succession Act 1965, unless a contrary intention appears in any enactment, references to the estate of a deceased person include reference to both the real and personal estate of the deceased person. It is the estate which devolves, as opposed to a distinct personal or distinct real estate.

References in the subsequent provisions of this Act and in any subsequent enactment to the estate of a deceased person shall, unless the contrary intention appears, include references to both the real and personal estate of that deceased person.

[Succession Act 1965, s 14].

Section 6 of the Succession Act was amended by the Courts Act, 1981 s 4. The amendment, by way of substitution, deletes any reference to the "personal estate". Consequently the jurisdiction of the Circuit Court, in relation to an estate which consists wholly of personal estate, is now unlimited. The jurisdiction of the Circuit Court in relation to estates which consist wholly or partly of realty is limited to cases where the rateable valuation does not exceed £200.00

4.—Section 6 of the Succession Act 1965, is hereby amended by the substitution of the following subsection for subsection (3):

(3) Unless the necessary parties to the proceedings in a cause sign, either before or at any time during the hearing, the form of consent prescribed by rules of court, the Circuit Court shall not, by virtue of subsection (2), have jurisdiction where the estate of the deceased person, in so far as it consists of real estate of which, at the time of his death, he was beneficially seised or possessed, exceeds the rateable valuation of £200.

[Courts Act 1981, s 4].

This act in turn was amended by the Civil Liability and Courts Act 2004, s 47 which amended the jurisdiction of the Circuit Court to an upper limit where the realty of the estate had a market valuation exceeding €3,000,000.

If the estate consists wholly of personal estate, the jurisdiction is unlimited.

47.—Section 6 of the Succession Act 1965 is amended by –

(*a*) the substitution, in subsection (3) (inserted by section 4 of the Act of 1981), of –

(i) "market value" for "rateable valuation", and

(ii) "€3,000,000" for "£200",

And

(*b*) the insertion of the following subsection:

(5) In this section 'market value' means, in relation to land, the price that would have been obtained in respect of the unencumbranced fee simple were the land to have been sold on the open market, in the year immediately preceding the bringing of the proceedings concerned, in such manner and subject to such conditions as might reasonably be calculated to have resulted in the vendor obtaining the best price for the land.

This Section has not yet been enacted by Statutory Instrument and therefore the limit should be described as a market valuation of three million euro or a rateable valuation of two hundred euro.

Forms and Notices

Table of Contents

Form 1

In the Goods of _____ late of _____ (address and description) _____ deceased.

I, _____ of (address and description) aged eighteen years and upwards, make Oath and say, that I believe the paper writing hereto annexed, and marked by me to contain the true and original Last Will (or last Will with _____ Codicils) _____ of _____ late of (address and description) deceased; that same was made by the said _____ after attaining the full age of twenty one years, and that the deceased did not intermarry with any person after the making of the same; that I am (state relationship) of the said deceased and the sole executor (or as the case may be) in the said Will (or Will with _____ Codicils) named; that I will faithfully administer the estate of the said deceased by paying his just debts and the legacies bequeathed by his said Will (or Will with Codicils), so far as the same shall thereto extend and the law binds me; that I will exhibit a true Inventory of the said Estate and render a true account thereof, whenever required by law to do so; that the testator died at _____ on the _____ (where application is made in District Probate Registry add: and the deceased had at the time of his death a fixed place of abode at _____ within the district of _____) and that the whole of the estate of the deceased which devolves to and vests in his legal personal representatives amounts in value to the sum of (gross assets without any deductions for debts) and no more to the best of my knowledge information and belief.

SWORN etc.
This Affidavit is filed on behalf of the applicant by

Form 2

OATH FOR ADMINISTRATOR WITH THE WILL ANNEXED

In the Goods of _____ late of _____ (address and description) _____ deceased.

I, _____ of (address and occupation) aged twenty one years and upwards, make Oath and say that I believe the paper writing hereunto annexed, and marked by me to the true and original last Will (or Will with _____ Codicils) of _____ late of (address and description) deceased, and that the same was made by the said _____ after attaining the age of twenty one years, and that he did not intermarry with any person after the making of same, and that he did therein name as his executor _____ who predeceased the deceased (or as the case may be) and I am the (state relationship) of the said deceased and one of the residuary legatees and devisees (or as the case may be) and that I will faithfully administer the estate of the said by paying his just debts, and distributing the residue of said estate according to law and that I will exhibit a true inventory of the said estate and render a true account thereof, whenever required by law to do so; that the said deceased died at _____ on the _____ (where application is made in a District Probate Registry add: and had at the time of his death a fixed place of abode at _____ within the district of _____) and the personal estate of the said deceased is of the value of (the gross personal estate without any deductions for debts) and the real estate of the deceased which devolves to and vests in his legal personal representative amounts in value to (the gross current value as per the affidavit/letter of market value) and no more to the best of my knowledge information and belief.
SWORN etc.

Form 3

OATH OF ADMINISTRATOR

In the Goods of _____ late of _____ (address and description) _____ deceased.

I, _____ of (address and description), aged twenty one years and upwards, make Oath and say that _____ late of (address and description) deceased, died intestate (state here whether bachelor (or otherwise) and clear off all other parties entitled to grant in priority to applicant and state capacity in which applicant seeks administration) and I am the lawful (state relationship) of the said deceased; and that I will faithfully administer the estate of the said _____ by paying his just debts, and distributing the residue of said estate according to law and that I will exhibit a true inventory of the said estate and render a true account thereof, whenever required by law to do so; that the said deceased died at _____ on the _____; (where application in a District Probate Registry add: and the deceased had at the time of his death a fixed place of abode at within the district of _____); and that the personal estate of the said deceased is of the value of (the gross personal estate without any deductions for costs) and the whole of the real estate of the deceased which devolves to and vests in his legal personal representative amounts in value to (the gross current value as per the affidavit/letter of market value) and no more to the best of my knowledge information and belief.

SWORN etc.

Form 4

ADMINISTRATION BOND

I, _____ of (address and description) _____ am liable in full to pay to the President of the High Court the sum of (double gross current value of assets without deductions for debts) for which payment I bind myself and my executors, administrators and successors.

Sealed with my seal
and dated the _____

The condition of this obligation is that if the above named the (indicate capacity in which applicant is applying for the Grant) of (name, address and occupation of the deceased), and the intended administrator/administratrix of the estate of the said deceased, do, when lawfully called on in that behalf, make or cause to be made a true inventory of the said estate which has or shall come into his/her hands, possession or knowledge, or into the hands possession or control of any person for him/her; do exhibit the said inventory or cause it to be exhibited in the Probate Office (or in the District Probate Registry in _____) _____ whenever required by law to do so; do well and truly administer the said estate according to law, paying all the debts owing by the deceased at the time of his/her death, all death duties payable in respect of the estate of the deceased for which the personal representative is accountable and all income and surtax payable out of the estate, distributing all shares in the estate to those entitled by law thereto and as the law requires; and further do make or cause to be made a true account of the administration whenever required by law to do so; and further do, if so required, render and deliver up the letters of administration in the High Court if it shall be thereafter appear that any Will was made by the deceased which is exhibited in the said Court with a request that it be allowed and approved accordingly; then this obligation shall be void and of no effect, but shall otherwise remain in full force and effect.

SIGNED SEALED AND DELIVERED
Etc.

Form 5

PRECEDENT AFFIDAVIT OF DUE EXECUTION
AND MENTAL CAPACITY BY SOLICITOR

THE HIGH COURT
PROBATE

In the estate of _____ late of _____ in the County of _____ deceased.

I, _____ of _____ in the County of _____ Solicitor, do hereby make oath and say as follows:

1. I am a Solicitor in the firm of _____ who are the Solicitors who acted for THE DECEASED and I make this Affidavit from facts within my own knowledge save where otherwise appears and where so appearing I believe those facts to be true.

2. I say that I am one of the subscribing witnesses to the Last Will of the said _____ deceased bearing the date the _____ and that the said Testator executed the said Will on the day of the date thereof, by signing his name at the end as the same now appears thereon, in the presence of me and of _____, Solicitor, the other subscribing witness thereto, both of us being present at the same time and we thereupon attested and subscribed to the said Will in the presence of the said Testator and of each other.

3. I say that I was the Solicitor who took instructions from _____ and I drafted and had engrossed the Will and arranged for the execution of same.

4. I say that I had ample time to study _____ the deceased and I say that I had no concerns as to his mental capacity in giving me instructions as to the contents of the Will. I say that as will be noted the Will devised two thirds of the Estate to one child and one third between the other two children and I say that _____ the deceased was quite clear in his instructions to me on this. I say that at no time did I detect any notice of confusion on his part and I had no apprehension as to his capacity to give instructions for the preparation of the Will.

5. From my enquiries I have ascertained that the doctor who was attending the said _____ deceased at the time he made his will was Doctor _____ of _____and that he died on the day of _____

SWORN etc.

Form 6

PRECEDENT AFFIDAVIT OF MENTAL CAPACITY BY DOCTOR

THE HIGH COURT
PROBATE

In the estate of _____ late of _____ in the County of _____ deceased.

I, _____ of _____ in the County of _____ Medical Doctor, do hereby make oath and say as follows:

1. I am medical doctor carrying on practice at _____ in the County of _____. I make this affidavit from facts within my own knowledge save where otherwise appears and whereso appearing I believe those facts to be true.

2. The above named _____ was a patient of mine for a period of fifteen years between _____ and _____.

3. I say and believe that I have been informed that he executed his last will and testament on the _____ day of 20___. I am quite satisfied that he was of sound disposing mind on that date and fully capable of making his will.

SWORN

Form 7

AFFIDAVIT OF DUE EXECUTION ILLITERATE
TESTATOR

THE HIGH COURT
PROBATE

In the estate of _____ late of _____ in the County of
_____ deceased.

I, _____ of _____ in the County of _____ Solicitor, do
hereby make oath and say as follows:

1. I am a Solicitor in the firm of _____ who are the Solicitors
   who acted for THE DECEASED and I make this Affidavit from
   facts within my own knowledge save where otherwise appears
   and where so appearing I believe those facts to be true.

2. I say that I am one of the subscribing witnesses to the last will
   [*or* codicil] of the said late of [*address and description*] deceased;
   the said will *or* codicil] bearing date the day of 20___, and
   that the said testator executed the said will [*or* codicil] on the
   day of the date thereof, by affixing his mark, being illiterate
   [*or* unable to write from physical debility], at the foot or end
   thereof as the same now appears thereon, in the presence of
   me and of the other subscribed witness thereto, both of us
   being present at the same time – and we thereupon attested
   and subscribed the said will [or codicil] in the presence of
   the said testator and of each other, And I further say, that
   before said testator executed said will [*or* codicil] in manner
   aforesaid, same was truly, audibly, and distinctly read over to

him by me, and said testator appeared fully to understand the same, and was at the time of the execution thereof of sound mind, memory, and understanding.]

SWORN

Form 8

AFFIDAVIT OF DUE EXECUTION BLIND
TESTATOR

THE HIGH COURT
PROBATE

In the estate of _____ late of _____ in the County of _____ deceased.

I, _____ of _____ in the County of _____ Solicitor, do hereby make oath and say as follows:

1. I am a Solicitor in the firm of _____ who are the Solicitors who acted for [*the deceased*] and I make this Affidavit from facts within my own knowledge save where otherwise appears and where so appearing I believe those facts to be true.

2. I say that I am one of the subscribing witnesses to the last will [*or* codicil] of the said _____ late of [*address and description*] deceased; the said will *or* codicil] bearing date the _____ day of _____ 20___, and that the said testator executed the said will on the day of the date thereof, by signing his name at the foot or end thereof as the same now appears thereon, in the presence of me and of _____ the other subscribed witness thereto, both of us being present at the same time – and we thereupon attested and subscribed the said will [or codicil] in the presence of the said testator and of each other, And I further say, that before said testator executed said will [*or* codicil] in manner aforesaid, same was truly, audibly, and distinctly read over to him by me, and said

testator appeared fully to understand the same, and was at the time of the execution thereof of sound mind, memory, and understanding and I further say that at the time of execution of the said will the testator was blind and I and the said _____, the other subscribing witness, signed our names in such a position that had the testator been possessed of his eyesight, he could have seen us sign.

SWORN

Form 9

PRECEDENT AFFIDAVIT OF PLIGHT AND CONDITION

THE HIGH COURT
PROBATE

In the estate of _____ late of _____ in the County of _____ deceased.

I, _____ of _____ in the County of _____ Solicitor, do hereby make oath and say as follows:

1. I am a Solicitor in the firm of _____ who are the Solicitors who acted for [*the deceased*] and I make this Affidavit from facts within my own knowledge save where otherwise appears and where so appearing I believe those facts to be true.

2. I say that I am one of the subscribing witnesses to the Last Will of the said _____ deceased bearing the date the __ _____ and that the said Testator executed the said Will on the day of the date thereof, by signing her name at the end as the same now appears thereon, in the presence of me and of _____, Solicitor, the other subscribing witness thereto, both of us being present at the same time and we thereupon attested and subscribed to the said Will in the presence of the said Testator and of each other.

3. I say that I have observed that there are staple holes and clip marks on the top left hand corner of the said will. I say that these staple holes and clip marks came about in the course of

the preparation of the will for probate when inadvertently the inland revenue affidavit was stapled to the said will and all the necessary documents were clipped together with a paper clip.

4. I say that nothing of a testamentary nature was at any time attached to the said will, which is now, except for the staple holes and clip marks, in the same plight and condition as when executed by the said testator.

SWORN, ETC.

Form 10

AFFIDAVIT OF MARKET VALUE

THE HIGH COURT
PROBATE

In the estate of _____ late of _____ in the County of _____ deceased.

I, _____ of _____ in the County of _____ Auctioneer/Valuer/Solicitor, do hereby make oath and say as follows:

1. I am acquainted with the value of lands in the vicinity of _____ in the County of _____ where lands belonging to the said _____ deceased are situate.

2. I have inspected the lands and holding of the deceased at _____ and in my opinion the said lands and holding would, on the date of the swearing hereof, have been of the value of about €_____ if then offered for sale on the open market.

SWORN

Form 11

RENUNCIATION OF PROBATE OR ADMINISTRATION WITH THE WILL ANNEXED

THE HIGH COURT
PROBATE

In the estate of _____ late of _____ in the County of _____ deceased.

Whereas (name deceased) died on the day of _____ *[where application is made in a District Probate Registry, add* having at the time of his death a fixed place of abode at _____ within the district of _____] and whereas, he made and duly executed his last will [*or* will and _____ codicils] bearing date the _____ day of _____ 20___, and thereof appointed I, the said _____ and _____ executors [*or as the case may be*].

Now I, the said _____ aged 18 years and upwards, do declare that I have not intermeddled with the estate of the said deceased, and will not hereafter intermeddle therein, with the intent to defraud creditors, and I do hereby expressly renounce my right to probate of the said will [*or* will and codicils], [*or* to letters of administration with the said will [*or* will and codicils] annexed] of the estate of the said deceased.

Dated

(Signed)

Form 12

PROBATE

In the estate of _____ late of _____ in the County of _____ deceased.

Let nothing be done in the estate of *A.B.*, late of _____ deceased, who died on the _____ day of _____ at _____ OR unknown to me [*E.F.* being the solicitor of] _____ *C.D.*, of _____ in the County of _____ having interest.

[Signed] *E.F*

[*Registered place of business*].

or C.D.,

[*Address for service*]._____

Form 13

CITATION TO ACCEPT OR REFUSE ADMINISTRATION

THE HIGH COURT
PROBATE

In the estate of _____ late of _____ in the County of _____ deceased.

Whereas, it appears by an affidavit of _____ of _____ filed in the Probate Office on the _____ day of _____ 20__ c, that you are the lawful [*spouse, civil partner, child, or as the case is*] and only next-of-kin of the said _____ deceased, intestate, who died on or about the _____ day of _____ 20__, and that [*party issuing citation*] claims to be [*state interest as creditor, next-of-kin (giving relationship*)], &c.].

NOW THIS IS TO COMMAND YOU, that within fourteen days after service hereof on you, inclusive of the day of such service, you appear in the Probate Office, personally, or by your solicitor, and accept or refuse letters of administration of the estate of the said deceased, as of a person dying intestate, otherwise to show cause, if any, why the same should not be granted or committed unto the said

Dated
(Signed)
Probate Officer.

Solicitor for said

[*Registered place of business*]._____

Form 14

CITATION TO ACCEPT OR REFUSE THE BURDEN OF THE EXECUTION OF A WILL

THE HIGH COURT
PROBATE

In the estate of _____ late of _____ in the County of _____ deceased.

To

Of

Whereas it appears by an affidavit of *A.B.*, of _____ filed in the Probate Office on the _____ day of _____ 20__, that you _____ are the executor, and you _____ the residuary legatees named in the last will of _____ late of who died on _____ and you _____ are his natural and lawful children, and only next-of-kin him surviving, and you _____ are the legatees named in his said will, and that the said *A.B.* claims to be a creditor of the said deceased [*if not a creditor, state his interest*] and desires to have a representative raised to the said deceased.

NOW THIS IS TO COMMAND YOU that within fourteen days after service hereof on you, inclusive of the day of such service, you appear in the Probate Office personally, or by your solicitor; you _____ the said [*executor*] to accept or refuse the burden of the execution of the said will; and in case you refuse the same, then you the said _____ [*the residuary legatees*], to accept or refuse letters of administration of the estate of the said deceased, with his said will annexed; and in case you decline same, then [*so on as to next-of-kin and legatees*], otherwise to show cause, if any, why letters of administration of the estate, with said Will annexed, of the said deceased, should not be granted to the said A.B.

Dated
(Signed)
Probate Officer.

Solicitor for the said *A.B.*

[*Registered place of business.*]

Form 15

AFFIDAVIT TO LEAD TO A CITATION

THE HIGH COURT
PROBATE

In the estate of _____ late of _____ in the County of _____ deceased.

I, _____ of _____ in the County of _____ do hereby make oath and say as follows:

1. The above named (deceased) late of in the County of (*description*), died on the _____ day of _____ 20__, having duly executed his last will on the _____ day of _____ 20__. I beg to refer to a copy of the said will upon which marked with the letter "A" I have signed my name prior to the swearing hereof.

2. In the said will: the testator thereby named (name executor) as sole executor and devised and bequeathed me (here set out the gift to the deponent).

3. The said (name executor) has neglected or refused to extract a grant of Probate of said will as a result of which I have been unable to obtain the said bequest.

4. By letters dated the day of and day of my solicitors Messrs have requested the said (name executor) to extract a grant of probate of the said will. I beg to refer to copies of the said letters pinned together and upon which marked with the letter

"B" I have signed my name prior to the swearing hereof. I say that not reply has been received to this correspondence.

5. I therefore pray for the issue of a citation to the said (name executor) to accept or refuse a grant of probate of the said will.

SWORN

Form 16

NOTICE OF RIGHT OF ELECTION UNDER
SECTION 115 WHERE DECEASED SPOUSE/
CIVIL PARTNER DIES WHOLLY TESTATE

In the estate of _____ late of _____ in the County of _____ deceased.

1. We _____ (name personal reps), being the personal representatives of the above named who died on the day of 20___ (the deceased) and probate of whose will issued forth to us from the Probate Office on the day of 20___ hereby give notice to you, being the surviving spouse/civil partner of the said deceased, pursuant to section 115 of the Succession Act 1965 (the act) as follows:

2. Under the terms of the will of the deceased he devised and bequeathed to you the following property on the terms set out as follows: (here set out exactly the devise and bequest under the will) in the will, copy of which is attached. The said devise and bequest was not expressed to be in addition to your legal right share in the estate under section 111 of the act.

3. Pursuant to section 115 of the act you may elect to take the devise and bequest outlined above or your legal right share.

4. In default of election you will be entitled to take the devise and bequest under the will and not the legal right share.

5. The right of election given to you pursuant to section 115 of the act shall not be exercisable by you after the expiration of six months from the receipt by you of this notice or one year

from the date of the grant of probate in the deceased's estate which is the day of 20___ whichever is the later.

Dated the day of 20___

Signed _____
Executors

Form 17

NOTICE OF RIGHT OF ELECTION UNDER
SECTION 115 WHERE DECEASED SPOUSE/
CIVIL PARTNER DIES PARTLY TESTATE

In the estate of _____ late of _____ in the County of _____ deceased.

1. We _____ (name personal reps), being the personal representatives of the above named who died on the day of 20___ (the deceased) and probate of whose will issued forth to us from the Probate Office on the day of 20___ hereby give notice to you, being the surviving spouse/civil partner of the said deceased, pursuant to section 115 of the Succession Act 1965 (the act) as follows:

2. Under the terms of the will of the deceased he devised and bequeathed to you the following property on the terms set out as follows: (here set out exactly the devise and bequest under the will) in the will copy of which is attached. The said devise and bequest was not expressed to be in addition to your legal right share in the estate under section 111 of the act.

3. The deceased died intestate in respect of the following property (here set out in detail the intestate property and its value). You are entitled to (all or two thirds) of such property.

4. Pursuant to section 115 of the act you may elect to take the devise and bequest outlined in paragraph 2 above together with the share of the property not disposed of by the deceased under his will, outlined in paragraph 3, or the legal right share.

5. In default of election you will be entitled to take the devise and bequest under the will outlined in paragraph 2, together with the share of the property not disposed of by will outlined in paragraph 3 and not the legal right share.

6. The right of election given to you pursuant to section 115 of the Act shall not be exercisable by you after the expiration of six months from the receipt by you of this notice or one year from the date of the grant of probate in the deceased's estate which is the day of 20___ whichever is the later.

Dated the day of 20___

Signed _____
Executors

Form 18

NOTICE OF RIGHT OF APPROPRIATION

In the estate of _____ late of _____ in the County of _____ deceased.

1. We _____ (*name personal reps*), being the personal representatives of the above named who died on the day of 20___ (the deceased) and probate of whose will (or administration in whose estate) issued forth to us from the Probate Office on the day of 20___ hereby give notice to you, being the surviving spouse of the said deceased, pursuant to section 56 of the Succession Act 1965 (the Act) as follows:

2. You are entitled to require us to appropriate to you under section 55 of the Act, in or towards satisfaction of any share of the estate to which you are entitled the dwelling, in which at the time of the death of the deceased, you were ordinarily resident, and also any household chattels.

3. If your share of the estate is insufficient to enable an appropriation to be made as aforesaid, the right conferred on you may also be exercised in relation to the share of any infant for whom you are a trustee under section 57 of the Act, or otherwise.

4. The right of appropriation conferred on you as aforesaid shall not be exercisable by you after the expiration of six months from the receipt by you of this notice or one year from the date of the grant of probate – Administration – in the deceased's estate which is the day of 20___ whichever is the later.

5. You are required to notify us in writing to appropriate the dwelling under section 55 of the act.

Dated the day of 20____

Signed _____
Executors

Form 19

RENUNCIATION OF SPOUSE/CIVIL PARTNER IN
THE MATTER OF THE SUCCESSION ACT 1965
SECTION 113/113A

Know all men by these presents that I _____ of _____ being
the lawful wife/husband/civil partner of _____ of _____
aforesaid DO HEREBY RENOUNCE pursuant to section 113/113A
of the Succession Act, 1965 (the act) my legal right to the his/her
estate to which I would be entitled under section 111/111A of the act
on the death of (name spouse/civil partner)

I confirm that prior to execution of this renunciation that I have
been advised by solicitor of the extent and effect of the said legal
right share.

Dated the day of 20____

Signed by the said
In the presence of:

Form 20

DEED OF DISCLAIMER TO ENTITLEMENT ON INTESTACY

This deed of disclaimer is made by me on the day of 20___ by me AB OF _____ address and occupation and description

WHEREREAS:

1. (named deceased) LATE OF (address and occupation) (hereinafter called "the deceased") died on the day of intestate.

2. The deceased died a married man with three children.

3. I am the lawful son of the deceased and I am advised that I am entitled to a one ninth share in the deceased's estate (hereinafter called "the share") under the rules for distribution on intestacy as set out in section 67 of the Succession Act, 1965 (the act).

4. I have not received any benefit, or any degree of beneficial ownership, control or possession from the share.

NOW IT IS HEREBY WITNESSETH that I hereby irrevocably disclaim absolutely any right, title or interest I may be entitled to in the share.

And I hereby acknowledge and confirm that I have been advised by solicitor that on the execution by me of this disclaimer I will lose any entitlement to the said share and further lose any right I may have to extract a grant of administration to the estate of the deceased.

IN WITNESS WHEREOF I have hereunto set my hand and affixed my seal the day and year first herein written.

Signed, sealed and delivered
By
In the presence of:

Form 21

DEED OF DISCLAIMER TO ENTITLEMENT ON DEATH TESTATE

This deed of disclaimer is made by me on the day of 20___ by me AB OF _____ address and occupation and description

WHEREAS:

1. (named deceased) LATE OF (address and occupation) (hereinafter called "the deceased") died on the day of testate.

2. The deceased died a widower with three children.

3. Under the terms of the will of the deceased, he devised and bequeathed to me the following property on the terms set out as follows: (here set out exactly the devise and bequest under the will) (the bequest).

4. I am advised that I am entitled absolutely to the property comprised in the bequest. .

5. I have not received any benefit , or any degree of beneficial ownership, control or possession from the bequest.

NOW IT IS HEREBY WITNESSETH that I hereby irrevocably disclaim absolutely any right, title or interest I may be entitled to in the bequest.

And I hereby acknowledge and confirm that I have been advised by solicitor that on the execution by me of this disclaimer I will lose any entitlement to the said bequest.

IN WITNESS WHEREOF I have hereunto set my hand and affixed my seal the day and year first herein written.

Signed, sealed and delivered
By
In the presence of:

Form 22

ASSENT AND APPROPRIATION IN FAVOUR OF
SURVIVING SPOUSE IN PART SATISFACTION
OF THE LEGAL RIGHT SHARE

THIS INDENTURE is made the day of 20___ and made between
of (hereinafter called "the personal representatives") of the one part
and of the surviving spouse of _____ the hereinafter described
testator (hereinafter called "the spouse").

WHEREAS:

1. _____ late of (hereinafter called "the testator") by his will
   dated the day of 20___ appointed the personal representatives
   as executors thereof.

2. The testator died on the day of 20___ and probate of the said
   will issued forth to the personal representatives on the day
   of 20___.

3. The testator left surviving him the spouse and three children.

4. The net value of the testators estate amounts to €3,000.000.00.

5. The value of the spouse's legal right share amounts to
   €1,000,000.00.

6. At the date of his death the testator was seised of the property
   described in the schedule hereto which property comprises
   the dwelling in which the testator and the spouse were ordinarily resident.

7. By notice dated the day of 20___ and served on the spouse the personal representatives notified the spouse of the right of the spouse to appropriate the dwelling and the household chattels in or towards satisfaction of any share of the spouse.

8. By notice in writing dated the day of 20___ the spouse notified the personal representatives of his/her desire to exercise the said right.

9. It is agreed between the parties that the value of the dwelling and household chattels is €800,000.00.

10. The personal representatives have agreed with the spouse to appropriate the dwelling and household chattels to her at a value of €800,000.00 in part satisfaction of her legal right share of €1,000,000.00 and the spouse has consented to the said appropriation as hereinafter appears.

NOW THIS INDENTURE WITNESSETH as follows:

1. The personal representatives in exercise of the power of appropriation conferred on them by the Succession Act 1965 and in exercise of the powers conferred on them as personal representatives and with the consent of the spouse hereby appropriate to the spouse the dwelling in part satisfaction in the sum of €800,000.00 of the spouses legal right share of €1,000,000.00.

2. For the purposes of giving effect to the said appropriation the personal representatives hereby assent to the vesting in the spouse of the dwelling in fee simple.

IN WITNESS WHEREOF the parties hereunto have set their hand and affixed their seals the day and year first herein written.

SCHEDULE

ALL THAT AND THOSE

ALSO INCLUDE A LIST OF THE HOUSEHOLD CHATTELS IF
NECESSARY

Signed, sealed and delivered
By
In the presence of:

Signed and sealed
By
In the presence of:

Form 23

ASSENT BY PERSONAL REPRESENTATIVES
UNREGISTERED LAND

THIS ASSENT is made the day of 20___ and made between of (hereinafter called "the personal representatives") of the one part and of (hereinafter called "the beneficiary").

WHEREAS:

1. _____ late of (hereinafter called "the testator") by his will dated the day of 20___ appointed the personal representatives as executors thereof.

2. The testator died on the day of 20___ and probate of the said will issued forth to the personal representatives on the day of 20___.

3. The said will contained the following devise to the beneficiary (here quote the devise from the will) of the property specified in the schedule hereto.

4. Now we the personal representatives hereby assent to the vesting in the beneficiary of ALL THAT AND THOSE the property specified in the schedule hereto for all the estate and interest of the said testator therein at the time of his death.

IN WITNESS WHEREOF the parties hereunto have set their hand and affixed their seals the day and year first herein written.

SCHEDULE

ALL THAT AND THOSE

Signed by the personal representatives
In the presence of:

Form 24

RECEIPT FOR A LEGACY

In the estate of _____ late of _____ in the County of _____ deceased.

I, _____ (*name beneficiary*) of hereby acknowledge receipt of the sum of €_____ from _____ (*name executor*) of the will of the above named deceased, through his solicitor Messrs., Solicitors, in full payment of a legacy to me under the will of the deceased expressed in the following terms:

> "the sum of €____ to my nephew John O'Sullivan of for his own use absolutely"

And I hereby indemnify the said executor against any claims, demands, costs and expenses howsoever arising, on foot of the said legacy.

Dated the day of 20___

Signed_____

Index

NOTES

NOTES

NOTES

NOTES

NOTES

NOTES

NOTES

NOTES

NOTES

NOTES

NOTES

NOTES

NOTES

NOTES

NOTES